Maker-Centered Learning

Empowering Young People to Shape Their Worlds

Edward P. Clapp · Jessica Ross · Jennifer O. Ryan · Shari Tishman

Foreword by Ron Berger

Afterword by Wendy Donner

JB JOSSEY-BASS™
A Wiley Brand

Copyright © 2017 by John Wiley & Sons, Inc. All rights reserved.
Published by Jossey-Bass
A Wiley Brand
One Montgomery Street, Suite 1000, San Francisco, CA 94104-4594—www.josseybass.com

Jossey-Bass books and products are available through most bookstores. To contact Jossey-Bass directly call our Customer Care Department within the U.S. at 800-956-7739, outside the U.S. at 317-572-3986, or fax 317-572-4002.

Wiley publishes in a variety of print and electronic formats and by print-on-demand. Some material included with standard print versions of this book may not be included in e-books or in print-on-demand. If this book refers to media such as a CD or DVD that is not included in the version you purchased, you may download this material at http://booksupport.wiley.com. For more information about Wiley products, visit www.wiley.com.

Library of Congress Cataloging-in-Publication Data

Names: Clapp, Edward P., author. | Ross, Jessica, 1966- author. | Ryan, Jennifer Oxman, 1974- author. | Tishman, Shari, author.
Title: Maker-centered learning : empowering young people to shape their worlds / Edward P. Clapp, Jessica Ross, Jennifer Oxman Ryan, Shari Tishman.
Description: San Francisco, CA : Jossey-Bass ; Hoboken, NJ : John Wiley & Sons, 2016. | Includes bibliographical references and index.
Identifiers: LCCN 2016031587| ISBN 9781119259701 (pbk.) | ISBN 9781119263661 (epub)
Subjects: LCSH: Maker movement in education. | Active learning. | Student-centered learning.
Classification: LCC LB1029.M35 C53 2016 | DDC 371.39—dc23
LC record available at https://lccn.loc.gov/2016031587

Cover images: Top image, photo by Jeanine Harmon
              Bottom image, photo by Melissa Rivard
Cover design: Wiley

Printed in the United States of America

FIRST EDITION

PB Printing 10 9 8 7 6 5 4 3 2 1

Contents

Contents

Acknowledgments

This book is the result of a three-year research project called Agency *by* Design that was funded by the Abundance Foundation and conducted at Project Zero, a research center at the Harvard Graduate School of Education. The project has put us in touch with more talented and interesting people than we ever could have imagined, and this book would not have been possible without the generous contributions of scores of collaborators every step of the way.

To begin at the beginning, we would like to thank Stephen Kahn of the Abundance Foundation for his ongoing support, his enthusiasm, and his ever present creative spirit. Without him this work would truly not have taken the shape it did. We also want to thank Liz Kahn, whose early vision illuminated the way, and Wendy Donner, for her early and ongoing leadership of the Agency *by* Design project in the San Francisco Bay Area. We are also especially grateful to Emi Kane, Benita Kline, Hal Leventhal, and the Abundance Foundation Board of Directors, without whose support this project would not have been possible.

We are most grateful for the time, energy, and openness to new experiences expressed by the many members of the Temescal and Oakland Learning Communities, in particular Maite Barloga, Kurt Kaaekuahiwi, Reggie Richardson, and Ronnie Richardson at Claremont Middle School; Carla Aiello, Michelle Beal, Jennifer Dunn, Danielle Erwin, Kathy Hatzke, and Marian Woodside at Emerson Elementary School; Tatum Omari at North Oakland Community Charter School; Thi Bui, Raquel Franker, Carmelita Reyes, and Brooke Toczylowski at Oakland International High School; Tara Austin, Richard Fairly, Natalia Cooper, and Casey Fern at Oakland Technical High School; Beatriz Calderon-Rivera, Harriet Cohen, Jenny Ernst, Jeanine Harmon, Alex Kane, Tom Little, Ilya Pratt, Renee Miller, and Meena Srinivasan at Park Day School; and Ryan Lewis at 826 Valencia. We additionally owe our gratitude to the many maker educators who helped us pilot test early drafts of our thinking routines through their membership in the Agency *by* Design Learning Community. In particular, we would like to thank Mariah Landers at the Alameda County Office of Education in Hayward, CA; Bruce Hamren at the Athenian School in Danville, CA; Andrea Sachdeva at the Boston ArtScience Prize in Boston, MA; Jeremy Boyle and Melissa Butler at the Children's Innovation Project in Pittsburgh, PA; Rebecca Grabman at the Children's Museum of Pittsburgh, PA; Kurt Kaaekuahiwi at Claremont Middle School in Oakland, CA; David Clifford, Corinna Hui, and Kyle Metzner at the East Bay School for Boys in Berkeley, CA; Karen Wilkinson at the Exploratorium in San Francisco, CA; Peter McKenna and Duncan Wilson at the Fox Meadow School in Scarsdale, NY; Darlease Monteiro at the Global Learning Charter Public School in New Bedford, MA; Steve Teeri at the HYPE Teen Center in Detroit, MI; Gus Goodwin at King Middle School in Portland, ME; Aaron Vanderwerff at the Lighthouse Community Charter School in Oakland, CA; Steve Davee at the Maker Education Initiative in Oakland, CA; Andy Forest at MakerKids in Toronto, ON; Jaymes Dec at the Marymount School of New York in New York City, NY; Amos Blanton at the Massachusetts Institute of Technology in Cambridge, MA; Alison Rinner Fullerton at MsBiz in Nashville, TN; Tatum Omari at North Oakland Community Charter School in Oakland, CA; Brooke Toczylowski at Oakland International High School in Oakland, CA; Mariano Ulibarri at the Parachute Factory in Las Vegas, NM; Jeanine Harmon, Jenny Ernst, Alex Kane, Renee Miller, and Ilya Pratt at the Park Day School in Oakland, CA; William MacFarlane and Bryce Taylor at Parts and Crafts in Somerville, MA; Lisa Yokana at the Scarsdale High School in Scarsdale, NY; and Tobey Balzer, Vince Durnan, and Jeff Greenfield at the University School of Nashville in Nashville, TN. In addition to the thoughtful educators we worked with, we also extend our warmest gratitude to all of the educators and thought leaders who have generously shared their time, knowledge, and experience throughout the interview strand of this inquiry: Jeremy Boyle, Melissa Butler, David Clifford, Steve Davee, Jaymes Dec, Youssou Fall, Andy Forest, Gus Goodwin, Bruce Hamren, Peter McKenna, Pamela R. Moran, Jeff Sturges, Steve Teeri, Gever Tulley, Mariano Ulibarri, Karen Wilkinson, Duncan Wilson, and Susie Wise.

We would further like to express our appreciation to the people and places that invited us into their making, design, and learning environments and engaged us in informal conversations about the work they do, especially Molly Rubenstein at

Artisan's Asylum in Somerville, MA; Andrea Sachdeva at the Boston ArtScience Prize in Boston, MA; Ellen Hathaway, Justine Macauley, and Gever Tulley at the Brightworks School in San Francisco, CA; Jessica Hobbs and Catie Magee at the Flux Foundation in Oakland, CA; Michelle Hublinka and Parker Thomas at the Maker Education Initiative in San Francisco, CA; and Kim Saxe at the Nueva School in Hillsborough, CA. We would also like to thank the wonderful people we met at American Steel Studios in Oakland, CA; Breakwater School in Portland, ME; the Crucible in Oakland, CA; King Middle School in Portland, ME; NIMBY in Oakland, CA; and Tech Shop in San Francisco, CA. Thanks as well to Brad Gentile at Propel McKeesport, Pittsburgh, PA, for sharing his documentation of student work with us.

Many individuals have played a variety of important behind-the-scenes roles to bring our research on this project—and this book—to fruition. Among them are the host of talented graduate students we have had the privilege to work with as research assistants. We would like to especially thank Cami Gordon, Amy Hachigian, Raquel Jimenez, Sarah May, and Chandell Stone for their exceptional contributions to the ideas expressed in this book. We also thank Peter "Bridge" Bridgford and Gabrielle Santa Donato for pilot testing our nascent interview questions with us and Oskar Kelly, Samuel Rallis, and Max Ryan for serving as our youth tool testers whenever we needed to experiment with an emergent activity or thinking routine. We would like to also thank our colleagues Ron Berger for his inspiration and endorsement, Alex Coppola for his videographic wizardry, Melissa Rivard for helping us make the work of our project visible, Matthew Riecken for graphically organizing our ideas, Andrea Tishman for designing our iconic logo, Christina Smiraglia and Liz Dawes Duraisingh for supporting us with their methodological expertise, Carla Lillvik for serving as a research librarian guide, the CASIE team for helping us share our work with educators around the world through the Project Zero Perspectives conference series, and David Stephen for working so closely with our teacher partners in considering how to incorporate making and design into their learning environments. Of course, it goes without saying that our work on this project would not have been possible without the camaraderie and intellectual administrative support of our many colleagues at Project Zero. In particular, we would like to thank Faith Harvey, Jordy Oakland, and Dami Seung.

Acknowledgments

Though not directly involved in the inner workings of the Agency *by* Design research initiative, we additionally offer our thanks to the many friends of our project, including Karen Brennan at the Harvard Graduate School of Education; Kylie Peppler at Indiana University Bloomington; Tiffany Tseng at the Massachusetts Institute of Technology; Stephanie Chang, Lisa Regalla, and Dale Dougherty at the Maker Education Initiative; the Open Bench Project in Portland, ME; the Open Portfolio Project; Natasha Bhalla and Jim Reese at the Washington International School; the #makered Twitter community; and all of the passionate teachers who have attended our conference presentations and professional development workshop sessions across the United States and around the world.

As we look to the future, we would like to especially thank Wendy Donner, Ilya Pratt, Brooke Toczylowski, and Aaron Vanderwerff for carrying the Agency *by* Design torch forward and Jeff Evancho and Megan Cicconi for sparking enthusiasm for this work in new audiences.

We would like to additionally express our gratitude to our editor Kate Bradford and to all of her staff at Jossey-Bass, especially Lily Miller, Pete Gaughan, Connor O'Brien, and Haritha Dharmarajan. Last but not least, we would like to thank our families for all of the love, support, and patience they have offered throughout the process of writing this book. We are especially grateful to our spouses Angela Mittiga, Bryan Polashenski, Jake Ryan, and Bob Sowa.

List of Tables and Figures

Foreword

I live in a rural town where most of the roads are dirt, where there are no traffic lights or stores, where the firefighters are volunteer citizens. Other than homes, the town has few buildings: a town hall, a post office, a church, a bar, and a school. For 25 years I was one of the few teachers in our small public school; almost everyone in my town under the age of 50 is a former student of mine. Students from this school have done remarkably well, by almost any measure: test scores, college, careers, and adult lives.

Here is an important thing: students in the school spent much of their time making things. Students worked hard at literacy and math skills, knowledge of the world, just like at any school. But they did not focus that learning toward preparing for tests; instead, they used that learning to make great things. Mothers and fathers in this town, many of whom worked hard all day with their hands, took tremendous pride that their children were not just getting smart but also were developing a strong work ethic, problem-solving skills, and high standards for quality.

With almost no town employees beyond a two-person road crew, the students stepped in to help. They created demographic maps of housing and roads; they created field guides to local species; they created books to honor the lives of local veterans, workers, and citizens; they created scientific reports of home radon levels, water quality in home wells, water quality in streams; they built recycling sheds and playground structures; they created road signs and public art. They were building the same academic skills as students in other schools, but with much deeper purpose and passion.

Today, that *passion in making great things* suffuses the national school network where I now work—EL Education—which comprises over 150 public schools across 30 states, some of which are featured in this book. Most of these schools are situated in low-income urban settings, and the results of this approach to learning are profound. Many of these schools, sited in cities where high school graduation rates are alarmingly low, are getting almost every student to graduation on time and getting every single graduate into college every year. Other school networks that share this approach, such as the High Tech High Schools in California, are getting these same results. This success is something we as a nation need to understand.

This book, *Maker-Centered Learning*, takes on the fundamental question of how *making things* connects to the learning process and to student empowerment. With depth, integrity, and insight that are hallmarks of Project Zero, this analysis of *making and learning* explodes the shallow binary debate about whether the new maker movement is a groundbreaking answer to transforming schools, or simply a distraction. It instead dives deeply into the questions no one is asking: *What constitutes "making"? How does the process of making instantiate learning? What are the characteristics of successful making experiences? In what conditions is making a transformational learning experience for students?*

This book is not an advertisement or an indictment of the maker movement but rather a balanced look at what the movement represents and where it lives in the educational landscape. The current movement, as this book points out, was primarily a white, male initiative centered on new technology that is now filtering into schools—disproportionately schools that serve economically privileged students. But the power of making things, within school and outside of it, is not in any way limited to this sector, and the underlying potential of a maker-centered pedagogy can cut across gender, class, age, and setting. Understanding the conditions in which making is transformative for children can improve learning during school and after school and can make makerspaces effective centers of learning.

Maker-Centered Learning should be required reading for any school or district that is considering building a makerspace. As an educator who has spent a lifetime focused on student craftsmanship, I am sad to say that I am as often depressed as inspired when I am brought into a contemporary school makerspace. It is not that a well-designed makerspace does not have potential. I have seen students creating originally designed, stress-tested, low-cost wheelchair components to be sent to a developing country. I was humbled. But much of the time when I enter a school makerspace I see students using 3-D printers to create sloppy plastic versions of their names, without purpose or craftsmanship. Those schools need this book.

But it is not that schools and districts need to read this book just to improve their new makerspace. Educators need to read this book to consider how we can elevate and support the power of maker-centered learning throughout the school day, in every classroom, and outside of school as well. To understand the conditions of learning in which students from all backgrounds can be engaged and supported to *make great things* and transform their learning and their lives.

Ron Berger, Chief Academic Officer, EL Education

Maker-Centered Learning

Introduction

In an old mayonnaise factory that has been repurposed as a tinkering school in San Francisco, California, a group of children measure, saw, and screw together wood planks and other building materials to make a functional ice rink that they fully expect to play hockey on within a matter of days. Meanwhile, across the country, unschooled and homeschooled students working in a storefront outside of Boston mash together an assortment of spare electronic parts to make tiny robots that scamper across the floor. While families in Detroit gather in a church basement after Sunday service to make snow globes out of household materials and learn the basics of bicycle maintenance, families in New Mexico visit rural libraries to learn how to connect fruits and vegetables to a device called a Makey-Makey. At the same time, visitors to a children's museum in Pittsburgh are learning the basics of electric circuitry alongside their siblings and parents. Back in California, first-generation public high school students work with their teacher to redesign their school's outdoor spaces, just as students at a private school around the corner research, design, and construct new furniture for themselves and their community. Across these disparate contexts, each of these learning environments provides a glimpse into an educational transformation that is sweeping across the United States—and around the globe.

The first Maker Faire, held in San Mateo, California, in 2006, marked a resurgence of interest in *making* things—as opposed to merely consuming them—while at the same time celebrating the gizmos and gadgetry of contemporary life. Since that event, small

1

and large-scale maker events have drawn crowds and inspired makers throughout the United States and around the world (Figure I.1). From basement workshops to massive cooperative makerspaces, interest in making has since been growing. Noting the significance of this trend, in 2014 the White House hosted its first ever Maker Faire and established June 18 as a National Day of Making.[1] In his address to the makers assembled for this historic event, President Barack Obama remarked:

> This is a country that imagined a railroad connecting a continent, imagined electricity powering our cities and towns, imagined skyscrapers reaching into the heavens, and an Internet that brings us closer together. So we imagined these things, then we did them. And that's in our DNA. That's who we are. We're not done yet. And I hope every company, every college, every community, every citizen joins us as we lift up makers and builders and doers across the country.[2]

Beyond the White House, scores of advocacy statements emphasizing the importance of making have spread throughout the media and the popular press.[3] As author and inventor Chris Anderson noted in his book *Makers: The New Industrial Revolution*, the next wave of manufacturing and entrepreneurship will be borne of the talents and shared ideas developed by makers.[4] A surge of voices from government, industry, and education further argued that to equip our young people for this next wave of entrepreneurship and innovation, it is important to support maker-centered learning in various educational environments. Whether in schools, after-school settings, libraries, or museums, an interest in providing opportunities and spaces for making has spread everywhere. This renewed interest in making has come to be known as the *maker movement*—a rising interest in sharing and learning from others while working with one's hands within interdisciplinary environments that combine a variety of tools and technologies.

Intrigued by the relationship between maker experiences, arts, and education, the Bay Area–based Abundance Foundation began to take notice.[5] With a deep commitment to public health, arts education, and empowerment initiatives, members of the foundation asked some compelling questions: What is the potential of bringing maker activities into educational settings? What might young people uniquely learn through maker experiences? What does making in schools currently look like? With these questions in mind, the foundation reached out to

Photo by Agency *by* Design.

FIGURE I.1: Young visitors to the 2014 World Maker Faire engage with an interactive LED exhibit at the New York Hall of Science.

Project Zero, a research center at the Harvard Graduate School of Education in Cambridge, Massachusetts, to see if there might be an opportunity to explore these questions together.

Project Zero was founded in 1967 by the philosopher Nelson Goodman to study and improve education in the arts. Goodman believed that arts learning should be studied as a serious cognitive activity but that "zero" had yet been firmly established about the field; hence, the project was given its name. Over the years Project Zero has maintained a strong research agenda in the arts while gradually expanding to include other areas of inquiry related to thinking and learning. With its current emphasis on interdisciplinarity, creativity, and multiple modes of learning, the maker movement presented an interesting opportunity for Project Zero to expand its research and to investigate if (and how) educational interventions could support maker-centered learning—and what their benefits might be. Thus, in spring 2012, backed by the support of the Abundance Foundation, the Agency *by* Design project was born.

Since its inception, the Agency *by* Design research team has endeavored to gain an understanding of the benefits of maker-centered learning and the pedagogies and practices that support it. To better understand this opportunity space, the Agency *by* Design team pursued three strands of inquiry: (1) a review of literature associated with maker-centered learning; (2) a series of site visits to a variety of maker-centered learning environments paired with formal interviews conducted with maker educators and thought leaders at the forefront of this emergent domain; and (3) a program of participatory research carried out first with a group of educators in Oakland, California, and later with a national learning community consisting of individuals representing maker-centered learning environments throughout the United States.

What the Agency *by* Design research team quickly discovered was that, while making in the classroom was not a new concept, maker-centered learning suggested a new kind of hands-on pedagogy—a pedagogy that encourages community and collaboration (a do-it-together mentality), distributed teaching and learning, boundary crossing, and responsive and flexible teacher practices. This book, *Maker-Centered Learning: Empowering Young People to Shape Their Worlds,* presents what our team has learned about this new pedagogical trend throughout our three years of research.

What Is a Maker? And What Is Maker-Centered-Learning?

As authors of a book titled *Maker-Centered Learning,* we feel responsible for articulating what we mean by *maker* and *maker-centered learning*. We recognize that some readers will arrive at this text with strong associations, and others may be unfamiliar with how they have come to be used. With this in mind, here and in the chapters ahead we have made a concerted effort to discuss maker-centered learning in a way that both invites newcomers into this landscape and also pushes the boundaries of what more-established maker-centered educators and advocates understand about this work. Whether readers of this book are members of the initiated, the uninitiated, or somewhere in between, we hope that the definitions offered will be illuminating for all.

For most people, the word maker conjures up images of people working with their hands—designing, building, and crafting. Seen in this light, maker is a noun: a way to describe someone who engages in the act of making, perhaps even a profession, like *artist* or *sculptor* or *crafter*. A maker might be someone who bakes bread or someone who quenches steel; she might be someone who builds chairs or someone who paints portraits. Ultimately, a maker is not a special title one achieves after gaining entry into an esoteric social club but rather is someone—anyone—who makes things. By understanding maker in this way, the maker community can be viewed as being inclusive, embracing, and welcoming to all those who make.

Often, though, a quick scan of the media coverage of the maker movement emphasizes a certain *type* of maker: hackers with expertise in robotics, information technology, and electronics, working with innovative tools and technologies such as 3-D printers, microcontrollers, and computer numerically controlled (CNC) tools. As designer, engineer, and educator Leah Buechley criticizes,[6] this narrow representation of makers places limits and constraints on the types of people who are identified as makers. To be more specific, she argues that the maker movement, as it has been portrayed in the popular press, can be seen as favoring the work and interests of white, middle-class males.[7]

Conjoining the terms maker with movement may add to the exclusivity of the phrase, because participating in a movement implies belonging and identity. As educational researchers Erica Halverson and Kimberly Sheridan note, the word maker "describes the identities of participation . . . that people take on within the maker movement."[8] Being part of a community implies being connected to its practices, norms, and responsibilities, which may leave some people wondering: Can I participate in this movement? Do I—or does my work—qualify me to be a part of this community? As Halverson and Sheridan argue, it is possible that a lack of identity with the dominant narrative presented by the maker movement may cause many would-be makers to feel alienated or self-select out of this growing cultural trend.[9]

Unfortunately, along with a sense of belonging comes the implicit corollary: not belonging. And this is where the label maker movement just might do itself a disservice. Putting boundaries around makers in the shift to *maker-as-cultural-identity* runs the risk of excluding those who might ordinarily consider themselves makers. Those bread bakers and chair builders might identify with other people who make things but not necessarily with the maker culture as it has been portrayed and promoted in the media.

Perhaps the making movement would have been a better name, capturing what people do rather than who they are. Yet there is something unique about the kinds of activities and culture in which the maker community engages. For instance, as our own research and the work of others has emphasized,[10] maker activities are inherently social as seen in the collaboration in Figure I.2. Community is an important aspect of participating in the maker movement—and the norms of that community are indeed important. So how can the maker movement and maker culture be framed more inclusively while also recognizing that the work happening in makerspaces and maker-centered classrooms has a distinct social ethos?

Photo by Melissa Rivard.

FIGURE I.2: Young makers constructing a trash collecting net for an environmental science exploration at Park Day School in Oakland, California.

One way to start is by explaining what we want the language we use to mean. Accordingly, we have developed a two-pronged way to address the definition of maker. First, we have reframed the kinds of activities we have been researching as *maker-centered*, with an explicit focus on learning (i.e., maker-centered learning). Second, we have taken a *symptoms-based* approach to defining what the maker in this context means.[11] Here we take inspiration from the founder of Project Zero, Nelson Goodman, who addressed the problem of defining art not by trying to identify the essence of art but rather by identifying several symptoms that are frequently present in works of art, none of which are disjunctively necessary for something to function as a work of art.

Each of these moves has allowed us to stretch the boundaries of maker. Maker-centered is more nuanced than just making (allowing for the uniqueness described already). A symptoms-based approach to defining the term helps us point to characteristics that suggest what qualifies as a maker-centered experience but that do not strictly define what the essence of such an experience is or is not. In other words, a maker-centered experience need not include the full set of characteristics associated with such experiences to qualify as one; rather, exhibiting a majority of these characteristics in any configuration will suffice.

Although such a symptoms-based approach can be applied to any kind of maker-centered experience, the Agency *by* Design research team's focus has been on learning. Through extensive conversations with educators and thought leaders at the numerous makerspaces, classrooms, and events we visited, patterns emerged that suggested a set of symptoms for what we began to understand as maker-centered learning. Specifically, three constellations of characteristics stood out as exemplifying typical maker-centered components: characteristics related to community, characteristics related to process, and characteristics related to environment.

Within the constellation of community characteristics, characteristics such as collaboration, distributed teaching and learning, the combination of diverse skills and expertise, and an expectation to share information and ideas all serve as symptoms of maker-centered learning. Within the constellation of process characteristics, curiosity-driven, experimental learning along with rapid prototyping, an interdisciplinary approach to problem solving, and flexibility all stand out as prominent symptoms of maker-centered learning. And within the constellation of environmental characteristics, open spaces, accessible spaces, and tool- and media-rich spaces all resound as symptoms of maker-centered learning.

With these three constellations of characteristics in mind, it is worth reiterating the symptomatic nature of our definition of maker-centered learning. No one learning environment exhibits all of the symptoms of maker-centered learning previously discussed, nor are these lists of symptoms exhaustive. Although the constellation of characteristics and their associated symptoms do bring maker-centered learning into relief, they are not meant to rigidly limit what may qualify as a maker-centered learning experience. By taking a symptoms-based approach, we have made it our goal to develop the most porous boundaries possible.

In much the same spirit, we have taken an inclusive approach to defining the settings where maker-centered learning takes place. Throughout this book we use the phrase maker-centered classroom to refer to the wide range of settings where young people and adults gather to engage in maker-centered learning experiences. Just as other researchers have noted,[12] maker-centered learning happens in a variety of different environments. These settings may include traditional classroom spaces in public, private, and charter schools, but they may also include libraries, museums, community makerspaces, afterschool programs, and everyday backyards, basements, kitchen tables, and garages. We use the term maker-centered classroom to embrace all of these environments.

A Road Map to the Journey Ahead

Maker-Centered Learning is structured around the three core questions that have been at the heart of the Agency *by* Design research initiative:

1. How do maker educators and leaders in the field think about the benefits and outcomes of maker-centered learning experiences?

2. What are some of the key characteristics of the educational environments and instructional designs under which maker-centered learning thrives?

3. What kinds of educational interventions can support thoughtful reflection around maker-centered learning and the made dimensions of our world?

Chapter One lays the groundwork for the rest of the chapters to come. It begins by drawing on the numerous conversations we have had with educators and thought leaders working at the forefront of maker-centered learning environments across the United States (and at one site in Canada) to address the first of our core questions: How do maker educators and leaders in the field think about the benefits and outcomes of maker-centered learning experiences? Looking at media coverage of the maker movement, visiting Maker Faires, and watching videos and tutorials from young stars like Super-Awesome Sylvia and Caine Monroy,[13] it is clear that young people can have a lot of fun making cool projects, and they can learn some useful technical skills along the way. But when educators talked about the deep and abiding benefits of maker-centered learning, it was neither the making of stuff they emphasized, nor the acquisition of technical or academic knowledge. Gever Tulley, founder of the Brightworks School in San Francisco, put it like this:

> *The world doesn't need more graduates with good grades: What the world needs is voracious, self-directed learners with the creative capacity to see the problems of the world as puzzles, and the tenacity to work on them, even in the face of adversity.*

As the interviews we conducted made clear, developing students' discipline-specific knowledge and skills (e.g., science, technology, engineering, and math [STEM] skills) and more maker-based knowledge and skills (e.g., learning to code or how to use a drill press) were certainly important to the educators we spoke with. But these learning outcomes were always discussed as being secondary or instrumental to the more dispositional outcomes of developing agency and building character. Chapter One presents these two primary benefits of maker-centered learning and discusses each in detail. We begin by examining what it means to develop a sense of agency—a proactive orientation toward the world. According to our interviews, maker-centered learning helps students see themselves as people who can effectively take action in the world, mainly—but not only—by making, hacking, or redesigning the objects and systems in their lives. Some educators characterized this agentic orientation as a set of life skills, like self-reliance and courage. Others described it as having the creative confidence to envision the world differently and take action toward that vision. With these views as a backdrop, this chapter discusses how developing a sense of agency can be understood in terms of *stuff making* and *community making*. While the former describes an inclination to make, hack, or redesign material objects, the latter suggests a similar orientation toward shaping or reshaping communities and social systems.

The chapter then goes on to discuss how maker-centered learning supports a sense of *self making*, or what we describe as building character. The character building that takes place in the maker-centered classroom can be described in terms of three kinds of achievements: building competence in the use of certain tools, materials, and processes; developing confidence in one's abilities; and ultimately developing an identity as a maker. Along the way, young people and adults further acquire a variety of general thinking dispositions. Like the sense of agency people develop through maker-centered learning, these general thinking dispositions can also be described in terms of *stuff making* and *community making*—both of which we discuss in detail.

Having identified the primary and secondary benefits of maker-centered learning in Chapter One, in Chapter Two we consider the various characteristics of instructional design that support these outcomes and the decisions educators make to achieve their learning goals. Drawing again on our interviews and site visits, Chapter Two addresses the core question: What are some of the key characteristics of the educational environments and instructional designs under which maker-centered learning thrives? The chapter examines what teaching and learning look like in the maker-centered classroom and what the maker-centered classroom looks like itself. We highlight the distributed nature of teaching and learning in these spaces, including the various roles that educators and students play, and the manner by which authority is redirected and distributed (Figure I.3).

Chapters Three, Four, and Five address the third core question of this book: What kinds of educational interventions can support thoughtful reflection around maker-centered learning and the made dimensions of our world? Chapter Three gives shape to a maker-centered perspective on agency. Here, we offer the concept of *maker empowerment*—a dispositional stance in which students understand themselves as individuals of resourcefulness who can muster the wherewithal to change

Photo by Melissa Rivard.

FIGURE I.3: In a tinkering class at Breakwater School in Portland, Maine, kindergarten students work together to build a geodesic dome.

their world through making. The chapter considers how we can help young people develop a sense of maker empowerment. It discusses the psychological elements necessary for dispositional development and suggests that an important but often overlooked component is developing a sensitivity to opportunity. In other words, to engage in dispositional behavior, one has to be sensitive to opportunities that invite or require that behavior.

This raises the question of how we can help young people to become sensitive to opportunities that activate their sense of maker empowerment. We turn to this question in Chapter Four and propose that to develop a maker-empowered disposition, students must first perceive elements of their world as inviting design. For example, they might think about redesigning a chair because they recognize that chairs are objects that can be reenvisioned and recrafted. This may sound simple, maybe even simplistic, but the truth is that we often go about life without paying much attention to the designed dimensions of objects and systems. For instance we use things like chairs and plates and soap dispensers without much thought; we participate in systems like lunch lines, food shopping, and electoral processes without paying attention to how they are designed or how they might be changed. This chapter argues that a key pathway to helping young people develop a sense of maker empowerment is to help them develop a sensitivity to the design of the objects and systems, large and small, that shape their worlds.

Chapter Five presents an instructional framework for maker-centered learning that centers on three critical maker capacities that support a sensitivity to design, which in turn encourages a sense of maker empowerment: (1) looking closely, which involves the careful observation of objects and systems to notice their intricacies, nuances, and details; (2) exploring complexity, which involves investigating the interactions between the various parts and people associated with objects and systems; and (3) finding opportunity, which involves seeing the potential for building, tinkering, re/designing, or hacking objects and systems. Chapter Five also draws on our collaboration with a teacher–partner group called the Oakland Learning Community, who have not only helped us develop the various tools described before but also provided us with important pictures of practice that illustrate what our instructional framework looks like in action. Lastly, this chapter presents several cognitive strategies—thinking routines—aimed at cultivating the capacity to look closely, explore complexity, and find opportunity. We begin by describing how thinking routines are generally designed to act as devices that elicit dispositional behavior. We then introduce the four thinking routines we have specifically developed to support having a sensitivity to design to foster maker empowerment.

In our concluding chapter we review the main themes of this book and look ahead to the future. Although this final chapter presents a positive outlook, we also candidly address the hurdles that lie ahead for realizing a more maker-empowered world. Here we consider the very real barriers to participating in maker-centered learning experiences that exist for the majority of young people and the biases that exist throughout the burgeoning field of maker-centered learning. The concluding chapter also considers the ethical dimensions of making. Maker-centered learning is frequently framed in a positive light, but it is important to note that the act of making may also involve serious ethical considerations that need to be addressed head on.

Finally, we put forth some *imagine if...* ideas of our own—imagining what a world of maker-empowered young people might be like, and further considering how the world might be a different place if each of us went about our daily lives with a more heightened sensitivity to design. Ultimately we conclude on a high note, returning to the benefits of maker-centered learning and emphasizing the potential for all young people to shape their worlds through building, tinkering, re/designing, and hacking.

In many ways, when the Abundance Foundation first approached Project Zero with an interest in developing a research initiative around maker-centered learning, we were transported back to Project Zero's roots. Just as there was little, or zero, communicable knowledge known about the cognitive affordances of the arts when Project Zero was founded in 1967, so, too, was there little communicable knowledge about the cognitive affordances of maker-centered learning when the Abundance Foundation first approached us in 2012. Several years later, we are happy to offer a research-based view of the benefits and outcomes of maker-centered learning, along with a pedagogical framework for bringing some of these about. We hope that this book will serve as a resource for the many educators, parents, and policymakers who have committed themselves to the work of empowering young people to view and shape their worlds through maker-centered learning.

Although we believe there is still much left to learn, we are delighted to present this book, *Maker-Centered Learning: Empowering Young People to Shape Their Worlds*, as an initial synthesis of our work—and as a celebration of maker educators, tinkerers, designers, builders, hackers, and doers all over the world.

Exploring the Benefits of Maker-Centered Learning

When the Agency *by* Design research project got under way in 2012, the buzz around the maker movement was on the rise, and discussions about the benefits of maker-centered learning were beginning to mount. New to this domain ourselves, our first instinct was to turn to the hundreds of short articles about the maker movement and maker-centered learning appearing in the popular press to gain a better understanding of the proposed benefits and outcomes of this new educational trend.[1] With titles like "School for Hackers," "Makerspaces in Libraries, Education, and Beyond," "Maker Spaces and the Learning Commons," and "DIY or Die: Why We Need to Teach Kids Practical Skills," the articles we reviewed discussed the application of maker-centered learning in a variety of settings—ranging from traditional classrooms to public libraries and from rural barns to the hallowed halls of the White House.[2]

Although each of these articles had its own way of talking about the promises of maker-centered learning, two prevailing narratives became evident. The first made the economic argument that maker-centered learning, and the broader maker movement, had the potential to reinvigorate the American economy and incite the next industrial revolution.[3,4] This narrative suggested that participating in the maker movement may help foster the development of an anticonsumerist, do-it-yourself mind-set on an individual level and spawn a wave of innovation and entrepreneurialism. On a more global level, the economic storyline further suggested that, through the use of new tools and technologies (particularly 3-D printers) and the adoption of an open-source culture, the maker movement also had the potential to entirely redefine contemporary corporate and manufacturing practices.

As powerful as this economic narrative was, all of this talk of anticonsumerism, economic growth, and disrupting corporate models began to feel a long way away from the tangible experiences of teaching and learning. So as we continued to review articles in the popular press, we listened closely for an underlying educational narrative as well. We heard it: This one had two primary strands. The first strand picked up on popular rhetoric advocating for the importance of teaching science, technology, engineering, and mathematics (STEM) by suggesting that maker-centered learning experiences have the potential to increase young people's proficiency in the STEM subjects.

Many advocates for developing the STEM proficiencies of young people through maker-centered learning experiences have rooted their arguments in alarmist cries from educational pundits and reformers who suggest that U.S. schools are failing to provide young people with the STEM learning experiences they need. These advocates further suggest that traditional textbook-based approaches to STEM learning are boring and uninteresting to young people. As noted by Margaret Honey, president and chief executive officer of the New York Hall of Science, "Marrying the passion, creativity, and engagement of the maker movement to educational opportunities that exist in formal and informal settings is the injection that STEM learning needs."[5]

Adding a sense of urgency to this message were reports that U.S. students lag behind other countries on standardized tests of STEM subjects and that there is a lack of young people pursuing higher education degrees in STEM content areas.[6,7] A recent report from the President's Council of Advisers on Science and Technology further stated that "the problem is not just a lack of proficiency among American students; there is also a lack of interest in STEM fields among many students."[8] So the second strand of the education argument makes the case that by engaging in maker-centered learning experiences—and in turn developing increased proficiency in the STEM subjects—young people are more likely to develop an interest in pursuing careers in the STEM fields. The educational narrative therefore circles back to the economic narrative by suggesting that supporting more students interested in the STEM professions today will help grow the American economy tomorrow.

These two narratives fit together neatly. Yet, despite their complementarity, we continued to feel that something was missing. Based on our early experiences visiting maker-centered classrooms and witnessing the vibrant teaching and learning going on within these spaces, we sensed that there was more to the story.

Learning from Maker Educators and Thought Leaders

Since almost the very beginning of our work as a research team, we have been offering workshops for educators and school leaders in which we share our ideas and build knowledge together with our workshop participants. When working with these professionals, we have often started such sessions with a thought experiment that goes like this: First, we ask our workshop participants to think quietly to themselves for a moment, identifying a memorable making experience from their past. After our participants have had a chance to orient themselves to such an experience, we then ask them to turn to a neighbor and discuss their memorable making experiences. After several minutes of lively conversation, participants share what they have discussed. Naturally, there is a great range of things people identify as being memorable about their past making experiences. Some popular responses include working closely with a family member or friend, figuring out the solution to a difficult dilemma, engaging in a real-world problem, or making something that was meaningful to oneself or one's community. So far, none of our workshop participants have described their most memorable making experiences in terms of reconceptualizing the economy or increasing their proficiencies in the STEM subjects.

The responses we have heard in these sessions have supported our skepticism about the rhetoric in much of the popular press. When we consider the benefits and outcomes of maker-centered learning on a human scale, we find that they are far more personal—and far more interesting—than the predominant economic and educational narratives suggest. So to gain a better understanding of the real benefits and outcomes associated with maker-centered learning, we decided we needed to ask the people who engaged in this work each day what they saw as the promises of this growing educational trend.

Our first core research question thus came into focus: How do maker educators and leaders in the field think about the benefits and outcomes of maker-centered learning experiences? To pursue an answer to this question, we interviewed a variety of maker educators and thought leaders from around the country to learn from their experiences and unique perspectives. (See Appendix A for a complete list.) Not surprisingly, our interviews yielded an impressive amount of data, which we carefully analyzed with the help of the many graduate research assistants we have had the pleasure to work with throughout this project.[9] We now turn to a discussion of the findings from this strand of inquiry.

Identifying the Real Benefits of Maker-Centered Learning

Just as our workshop participants identified maker memories that extended far beyond the economic and educational narratives prevailing in the popular press, the educators and thought leaders we spoke with talked of the promises of maker-centered learning as being greater than the media suggested. To be sure, these individuals mentioned proficiency in the STEM subjects as being a part of their work with young people, and naturally they wanted their students to be successful participants in the future economy. But as important as these outcomes may have been, they clearly were seen as being either instrumental or peripheral to greater learning objectives. Ultimately, we understood that the educators and thought leaders we spoke with discussed the outcomes of maker-centered learning primarily in terms of developing agency and building character. Agency and character can loosely be understood as being on a spectrum, on which one end is character building, or establishing a sense of self in a complex world, and the other end is developing agency, or activating one's character to uniquely shape one's world. The following section provides an explanation of these two primary outcomes. After that, we turn to the secondary outcomes our maker educators mentioned—outcomes that have to do with discipline-specific knowledge and skills, and maker-specific knowledge and skills. Although the primary outcomes of agency and character seem separate from the secondary outcomes of discipline- and maker-specific knowledge and skills, the two sets of outcomes are actually closely linked.

Understanding the Primary Outcomes of Maker-Centered Learning: Developing Agency and Building Character

Beyond cognitive capacities, maker-centered learning outcomes such as agency and character are dispositional in nature. They emphasize the propensity to see and engage with the world from the vantage point of a particular perspective rather than the acquisition of specific skills or proficiencies.

Developing Agency

One of the primary outcomes of maker-centered learning mentioned by all participants in our study—and talked about with passion—had to do with helping young people develop an I-can-do-it attitude. We have interpreted this can-do spirit as a sense of *agency*.[10]

Agency is a concept that is central to the eponymously named Agency *by* Design project and also to theories of human nature and development more broadly. In Chapter Three we explore the philosophical and psychological dimensions of the concept of human agency in more depth, but here we offer this simple definition: Having a sense of agency means feeling empowered to make choices about how to act in the world. In the context of maker-centered learning, agency has to do with action-based choices related to making. As such, agency, like character, can be understood as a disposition—seeing oneself as an agent of change within the designed environs of one's world.

The obvious connection between this conceptualization of agency and maker-centered learning concerns just what our interviewees pointed out—helping students develop an I-can-do-it orientation toward making tangible objects. Although the educators we spoke with did make this connection, they also believed that developing a maker-centered sense of agency means more. As we listened closely to how they framed the concept of agency, we discovered that they talked about the relationship between agency and making in two distinct but interrelated ways: making stuff and making communities.

A peek inside our participants' various classrooms, makerspaces, shops, and tinkering studios reveals all manner of materials and tools, along with projects in various stages of development. Visible are sketches, models, and drafts, shelves filled with paper, scrap wood, metals, and plastics. These working spaces have an inviting, student-centered feel, and virtually all of the educators we spoke with wanted students to feel at home in them and get excited about making personally relevant stuff (Figure 1.1). As Peter McKenna, an elementary school technology teacher at Fox Meadow Elementary School in Scarsdale, New York, explained, when students have a chance to mess around regularly in makerspaces, "they feel empowered to create something or fix something that may occur in their life."

Photo by Melissa Rivard.

FIGURE 1.1: Students in Tanya Kryukova's physics class at Lighthouse Community Charter School, in Oakland, California explore the physics of speakers.

Everyone we spoke with underscored the importance of the personal element in making stuff. They want their students to find opportunities to make things that are meaningful and to take ownership over the process of making. Having a sense of agency through stuff making builds on the can-do spirit, especially around feeling empowered to make choices about how to act in the world. For example, Bruce Hamren, a science teacher and maker educator at The Athenian School in Danville, California, talked about explicitly encouraging students to think deeply about how they make choices when they make things. He wants students to be thoughtful about choice so that the things they make will have qualities that reflect their own personal values, for instance by being precise, beautiful, or functional. Bruce believes that this connection to personal values is key in encouraging students to have the feeling of "I can do that or I know how to approach that."

As Bruce's viewpoint suggests, encouraging students to develop a sense of agency about stuff making has as much to do with helping them take ownership of the process of making as it does about helping them make actual stuff. Much of the time, this means helping students develop a sense of agency around figuring out how to make or fix things rather than simply relying on their teachers to tell them step by step what to do. Jaymes Dec, the Fab Lab coordinator at Marymount School of New York in New York City, put it this way: "I don't want to give students the code, and give them the design for a project and say, 'Build this.' I want them to work up to it and feel ownership over a project."

This sense of owning the process often extends to the very framing of the problem to be solved through making. Recalling a student's approach to an inventions class project, Andy Forest, founder of MakerKids in Toronto, told a story that vividly illustrated this point:

> There's a girl who had trouble getting up in the morning. So as an adult, my first thought was to suggest a project to make a creative way to wake her up. "Let's put a cold cloth on your feet," or something like that. But her problem was that it was too cold in the morning and she was snuggled up in her bed and it was nice and cozy. She didn't want to get out of a nice, warm bed. So brainstorming some more and more expanded that problem into an idea that she created. Out of plumbing pipes that she drilled holes into, she made a mannequin to put her clothes on. She then hooked a heater up to a timer and

connected it to the mannequin, so that 15 minutes before her alarm went off in the morning, the heater would turn on, force air through the pipes—and warm up her clothes. That's how she directly solved her problem in her own way.

When Andy told this story, his delight and pride as an educator clearly came from the student's personalization and originality of vision, not just from her technical accomplishment. As he said with a broad smile, she "solved her problem in her own way."

In addition to the agency around making stuff, the educators we interviewed also talked about encouraging students to develop a sense of agency related to their community. Paralleling the definition of agency as stuff making, agency as community making can be defined as finding opportunities to make things that are meaningful to one's community and as taking ownership over that process of making either independently or with others.

When the concept of community is discussed in connection with the maker movement, it usually refers to the strong sense of community among makers. For example, it is often used to characterize the spirit shared by makers of every stripe and age that gather at Maker Faires. These large-scale show-and-tell events are a wonderful example of a sense of maker community writ large. Here, though, we point to a somewhat different sense of community: the sense of being empowered to create change within one's community.

As noted by Jeff Sturges, conductor of the Mt. Elliott Makerspace in Detroit, Michigan, "Part of fostering agency is helping people understand that they have the power to make change both in their own lives and in the world around them." Indeed, it is this sense of empowerment with regard to effecting change in one's community that many of the participants in our study discussed.

We further found that when our maker educator colleagues discussed agency in the context of community making, they frequently talked about the importance of building communities and caring for one another within those communities. Gever Tulley, founder and education architect of the Brightworks School in San Francisco, California, spoke at length about the importance of developing the capacity to care for one another in the maker-centered classroom:

When you take on a project and you have peers on that project, teammates essentially, that social negotiation that comes in so many different ways, whether it's coming to a consensus about what color to paint the car you've just built or talking about what you're trying to say at this moment in the play and why this scene is important and all those nuanced little negotiations of listening to somebody else's ideas and incorporating them and caring for their social and emotional wellbeing as well as your own. You're not responsible for them, but you have to take care with them. You have to understand the impact that your words can have on them or that your actions can have on them. And I think giving them a place where they can see the value in that concretely helps them quickly take those steps of responsibility of caring for people. That's really at the heart of it, is that we should all care for each other.

Steve Davee, director of education at the Maker Education Initiative in Oakland, California, likewise placed an emphasis on the caring that takes place when young people engage in maker-centered learning. From Steve's perspective, caring is innate: "It's built into kids to want to care for things," he said. "They play with dolls, they care for each other when they play, they're constantly taking on this role of parenthood, adulthood, friendship, that type of stuff. It's built in, this instinct to take care of each other." The trick, Steve suggested, is figuring out how to incorporate a young person's natural inclination to care into their work in the maker-centered classroom. "How do you recognize that?" he asked, "how do you capture it, make it real and tangible through making and then put it back out there as something that is connected to something you can investigate in the world?"

For both Gever and Steve, caring for community includes a sense that one's actions, and the things one makes, have implications for others. "I think it really does come down to seeing your own actions as greatly affecting those of the community," Steve said. Reflecting on the goals he and his colleagues have for their students, Gever noted that community can stretch beyond the walls of the maker-centered classroom and that making can have a social purpose. Referring to his Brightworks students, he said, "I think another characteristic we would like them to have when they graduate is a sense of responsibility to those around them and the world. Even if it's locally focused, it's just that they feel like they are a member and a part of society and that they have a responsibility there to do right."

We heard another example of the importance of developing this kind of social agency from Pam Moran. Pam is the superintendent of schools in Albemarle County, a region in the heart of central Virginia that includes rural, suburban, and urban schools, where she has long been an advocate of project-based learning, particularly in nontraditional settings. So when the maker movement came along, Pam was a natural ally. With Pam's encouragement, some of the middle schools in her district created what they call Spark Spaces—cubbies and corners in the school that have been refashioned into places where cross-grade-level students come together to work on projects of their choice. In one of these spaces, students had made organic gardens. Not long before we interviewed Pam, she had decided to pay students a visit in one of the Spark Spaces. In our interview, she explained that she found the students making preparations for a walk they were planning to take through a local mall on the weekend, to promote organic farming in their community. The students were hard at work making signs and designing outfits to wear. Their energy and excitement was palpable. As Pam put it, "the research that they'd done and the ideas that they have generated, and the project that came out of that, in terms of their agency and advocacy, was pretty phenomenal. And it was so kid-owned." As Pam reflected later, for these kids, it was not just learning to make things, it was "learning in order to have influence."

Pam's story resonates with much of what we heard from other participants in our study. Many educators told stories about students aiming to make a difference in their communities through making. Youssou Fall, a technical arts teacher at Lick-Wilmerding High School in San Francisco, California, asks his students to investigate the needs of local public outdoor spaces, and design and build outdoor furniture with these needs in mind. Across the San Francisco Bay, David Clifford—a former Lick-Wilmerding educator—is one of the founding directors of innovation and outreach at the East Bay School for Boys in Berkeley. David's students investigate the needs of local community members, such as the homeless population, and then consider what they can make to help out those individuals.

Speaking about the broad goals of maker-centered learning, Steve Davee said, "It's really not about the technical skills. It's more about how students see themselves and how that reflects upon others. So it's really about the sense of empowerment.

It's not even self-esteem, it's more of a self-competence—seeing themselves as contributing members of society, with empathy to recognize the interests of others, and to reach out and help."

Few may argue with the value of encouraging young people's impulse to reach out and help. But it is fair to worry that unless such impulses are connected to a concrete and sometimes difficult understanding of real human needs, they can foster a generalized, feel-good empathy that tilts toward stereotype and a savior mentality.

David Clifford told a story that nicely illustrated this. As mentioned already, his students wanted to make something to help the homeless people in their community. They came up with the idea of making hooks that could attach to shopping carts to make it easier for homeless people to carry their belongings around. David explained that the boys "made particular assumptions about the homeless, including the homeless across the street." However, when the students began the process of actually making the hooks, they realized they needed more information. So they went out to interview some homeless people in the neighborhood to determine whether they were fulfilling a need or not. David pointed out that the making process—the process of designing and blacksmithing the hooks—ultimately sent students across the street to have a conversation with individual people. It turned out that if the hooks were of a specific design they could be more helpful for holding items and keeping clothes dry in the shower area at the local shelter. "That's inquiry," David said, proud that the students were able to ask the right questions. "Be observant of what's happening, and be open to the feedback." In this case, the initial feedback was, "I resent that you think that I use a cart to bring my stuff around. That's a stereotype." Students were able to surface and check their assumptions. In doing so, the sense of agency they developed around helping their community was strengthened, and made authentic, through making a connection to real people and real lives.

Building Character

In addition to developing agency through stuff making and community making as discussed already, the educators we spoke with also talked about a certain brand of self making that takes place in the maker-centered classroom. Students develop certain aspects of character that are deeply linked and inform the way they think and feel about themselves: building competence, building confidence, and forming identities.[11] They described this process of character building as unfolding something like this: When young people moved from baseline competency to more complex levels of ability, they developed an increased sense of confidence in their abilities. This building of confidence is closely related to developing a sense of identity in relationship to one's work in the maker-centered classroom. In other words, what may start out as simple skill building may soon turn into important identity building based on the confidence developed through one's maker abilities. It is here that an understanding of character building as a disposition-based outcome of maker-centered learning comes into focus: As a student begins to see herself not merely as someone who can make things but as a maker (or more specifically a Scratch programmer, knit bomber, or turntablist), she develops a new orientation toward who she is as an individual in the world (Figure 1.2).

Karen Wilkinson is director of the Tinkering Studio at the Exploratorium in San Francisco, California, and a widely respected authority in the maker-sphere. Like all of the maker educators we interviewed, she emphasized the importance of building competence and confidence, and she was especially interested in the contribution of these character traits to what she and her colleagues refer to as a tinkerer's disposition. She believes that developing confidence and competence help students become more comfortable with the natural uncertainties of the tinkering process. "Once you get comfortable and you have a tinkerer's disposition, you're much more willing to go into something without a clear goal in mind," she said.

Maker-centered competence and confidence may support the development of a tinkerer's disposition specifically, but they can also be seen as building blocks for a wide variety of other dispositions. For instance, as a result of building competence and confidence—and depending on the particular maker activities a student engages in—a student might develop a carpenter's disposition, an entrepreneur's disposition, a muralist's disposition, or a hybrid disposition that draws on a combination of any number of maker competencies.

In addition to building character through competence, confidence, and forming a maker identity, our interviews surfaced another kind of character building that

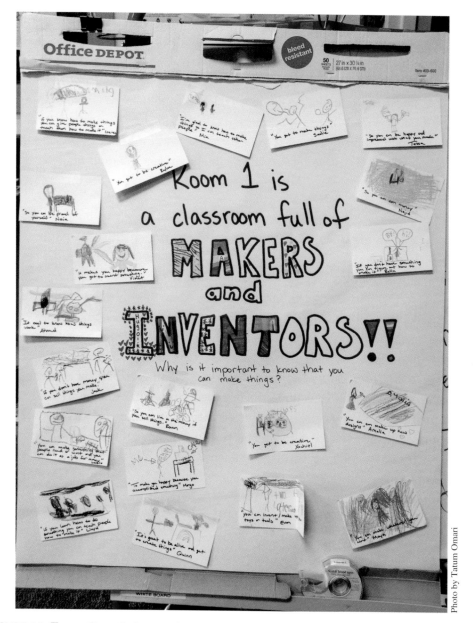

FIGURE 1.2: Tatum Omari's first-grade students at North Oakland Community Charter School express how they identify as makers and inventors.

takes place when young people engage in maker-centered learning experiences. During one of our discussions, Youssou Fall shared what his students say they learn through their work in his class: to be patient, to recognize how their limitations guide them through the making process, to collaborate, to work with their peers, to respect the material and the tools, and to develop a sense of common, shared projects. What Youssou's students say they learn captures the heart of something we seemed to hear from educators over and over again: the importance of fostering various general thinking dispositions through maker-centered learning.

Here, we use the term general thinking dispositions to refer to a host of capacities that readers will be familiar with—though perhaps under different names. Many readers will have heard the terms *soft skills, noncognitive skills,* or *twenty-first-century skills.* The qualities frequently mentioned within these various typologies refer to patterns of thinking that are viewed as being highly valuable but (a) lack specific associations with particular disciplines or domains and (b) cannot easily be measured with psychometric tests used to gauge cognition or intelligence. As Camille A. Farrington and her colleagues from the University of Chicago argued in a report on the effects of noncognitive factors on school performance, "In addition to content knowledge and academic skills students must develop sets of behaviors, skills, attitudes, and strategies that are crucial to academic performance in their classes, but that may not be reflected in their performance on cognitive tests."[12] These noncognitive skills (or factors, as Farrington and her colleagues call them) can be applied across domains and are of value in any number of contexts. Farrington and her colleagues have further argued that in many studies "noncognitive attributes are shown to have a direct positive relationship to students' concurrent school performance as well as future academic outcomes."[13]

But what might be the core set of noncognitive skills—or as we call them, general thinking dispositions—that make makers tick? Interested in a similar question, AnnMarie Thomas, an engineering professor at the University of St. Thomas, interviewed dozens of adult makers to gain a better sense of what, as young people, helped support them in becoming the makers they are today. Reporting on this inquiry in her book, *Making Makers: Kids, Tools, and the Future of Innovation,* Thomas identified eight attributes that she suggests are important to cultivate in young makers:[14]

- Makers are curious. They are explorers. They pursue projects that they personally find interesting.

- Makers are playful. They often work on projects that show a sense of whimsy.

- Makers are willing to take on risk. They aren't afraid to try things that haven't been done before.

- Makers take on responsibility. They enjoy taking on projects that can help others.

- Makers are persistent. They don't give up easily.

- Makers are resourceful. They look for materials and inspiration in unlikely places.

- Makers share—their knowledge, their tools, and their support.

- Makers are optimistic. They believe that they can make a difference in the world.[15]

In addition to Thomas, other researchers and advocates of maker-centered learning have begun to report on similar sets of noncognitive skills supported by making experiences, among them inspiration, collaboration, a growth mind-set, motivation, and the development of a failure-positive outlook on the world.[16] When talking about the outcomes of maker-centered learning, the maker educators we spoke with mentioned many of the same maker attributes. For example, Melissa Butler, codirector of the Children's Innovation Project in Pittsburgh, Pennsylvania, highlighted the importance of fostering curiosity as a general thinking disposition—or a habit of mind. "I want children to be curious, even if they're sitting on a chair and there's nothing outwardly around them," she said. "I want them to be curious about a piece of fuzz, or a wrinkle on their jacket. I want them to be curious in a way that, even if you stripped everything away, they would still have this capacity to be curious, to notice and wonder, and let their curiosity take them somewhere." Describing more than a skill, Melissa wonderfully emphasizes how curiosity can be cultivated as a disposition—as a way of seeing and being in the world.

In addition to curiosity and the many other general thinking dispositions that Thomas noted already, the maker educators we spoke with also suggested that divergent thinking, problem solving, critical thinking, inquiry, close observation and slow looking, cultural competency, and aesthetic sensitivity were among the many general thinking dispositions developed through maker-centered learning.

If you are feeling as though this long list of general thinking dispositions has begun to have a kitchen sink or laundry list feel to it, we agree. At times, our transcript notes on the general thinking dispositions mentioned during our conversations with maker educators looked quite a bit like a comprehensive inventory of effective thinking capacities. This may not be surprising given the vast array of general thinking dispositions that might come into play to carry out the work of making. But to be fair, this extensive suite of general thinking dispositions, whether in whole or in part, can just as easily be associated with arts education, vocational education, apprenticeship in the crafts, or any other form of hands-on, project-based, or problem-based learning.

Like Thomas, we were interested to see if maker-centered educators noted some unique thinking dispositions more than others. Indeed, several rose to the surface. As with the earlier discussion of agency, these included general thinking dispositions associated with stuff making, such as risk taking, persistence, learning from failure, and craftsmanship, and also general thinking dispositions more associated with community making, such as perspective taking and empathy.

When discussing general thinking dispositions associated with stuff making, our conversations with maker educators often referenced the hack-at-it and what-would-happen-if sensibilities of the maker movement. This experimental mentality parallels the risk taking general thinking disposition. With the belief that one's work is not precious and that there is always the chance to do it again, students are inclined to take chances and be bold in their actions, as shown in Figure 1.3. The maker brand of risk taking is supported by an emphasis on iteration in the maker-centered classroom; access to inexpensive, nonprecious materials; and a spirit of invention that pervades the maker ethos.

This risk taking is supported by persistence. In the maker-centered classroom, persistence involves "not stopping when you hit the first roadblock," as Youssou

Photos by Melissa Rivard.

FIGURE 1.3: Fourth graders engage in a toy take-apart activity, discovering how mechanized toys work while embracing the idea that "nothing is precious."

Fall suggested. Concerning his work with young people at Lick-Wilmerding High School, Youssou saw persistence enacted when his students endeavored to figure out solutions when faced with obstacles. "So hitting the first roadblock doesn't stop them," he said. "They have to have a desire to go deeper and say, 'I think I can do this. I was trained to do this. I think I can do it.' And then they push deeper." As Youssou suggested, persisting through difficulty leads to both a deeper and more intriguing next problem set and to a deeper understanding of the tools, topics, technologies, and materials at hand. Young makers understand that, although the journey might be arduous, the payoff is worth it.

Persistence aligns well with the concept of *grit* made popular by educational researcher Angela Duckworth, who defined it as "perseverance and passion for long term goals." More specifically,

> *Grit entails working strenuously towards challenges, maintaining effort and interest over years despite failure, adversity, and plateaus in progress. The gritty individual approaches achievement as a marathon; his or her advantage is stamina. Whereas disappointment or boredom signals to others that it is time to change trajectory and cut losses, the gritty individual stays the course.*[17, 18]

In much the same way that Duckworth and her colleagues describe, young people in the maker-centered classroom persevere in their pursuit of long-term goals. Work in the maker-centered classroom may not endure for the years and years that

Duckworth has suggested, but the concept of working through failure and adversity is, nonetheless, a character building skill associated with young makers.[19] In fact, some of the educators we spoke with intentionally designed their learning experiences to be challenging in just such a way. Melissa Butler spoke about this concept in terms of *struggle*. "You have to really talk about how struggle is good," she said, and then went on to describe how she and her colleagues design their work with young people to foster an environment that encourages their students to "think deeply and want to struggle." Developing an appetite for challenging activities that requires a degree of struggle, however, is not always easy—or immediately of interest—for many young people.

Mariano Ulibarri told a story that brings this point to life. Mariano is the founder of the Parachute Factory, a community makerspace in Las Vegas, New Mexico, out of which he runs traveling maker programs around the state. He focuses particularly on programs that reach youth in rural areas and connects them with one another through making. Like all of the maker educators we spoke with, Mariano is invested in supporting students' self-development. He told the story of Frederica,[20] whom he met when she was in fifth grade. "She was brilliant," Mariano exclaimed. "Everyone called her 'fun fact Frederica.' She loved talking about science, and she'd always have information about anything you'd mention." But what Mariano began to see over time was that Frederica was really insecure about *not* being perfect. "She knew people saw her as [perfect], so she was petrified of putting anything out into the world that wasn't absolutely perfect and well engineered." The consequences, Mariano explained, were extreme: "She failed at math in school. She failed in science—even though I knew she was brilliant." Eventually Mariano got Frederica involved in his Hacker Scouts program as a volunteer, where she spent a lot of time helping other kids learn by going through multiple cycles of tinkering, hacking, failing, and trying again. Eventually, Frederica began to muster the courage to start working on her own projects. "I've seen her change drastically in the last couple of years," Mariano said. "I'd like to think it was in part because of this. She started seeing everyone failing and pushing through it," he explained, "and she finally began to let go of the need to be perfect." Mariano recounted how Frederica talked to him about her feelings. "It was hard for me to get these projects started," she said, "because I felt like it was too much and I was not going to make it there, so I didn't even try." Mariano watched Frederica learn to push past this fear, and he could see her pride. He summed up her story this way:

> In the bigger picture, I think it's going to help her let go of some of those things if she can put things out there that aren't perfect. Take some criticism, I guess. Turn it into steps that she can take. And it goes back to that failing thing—failing is okay, it's part of the process. That's something that is going to be learned if you stick with this stuff. And it's going to be known inside of you. I think embracing failure is going to help her. We're already seeing her grades go up. We're already seeing her put more things out there, be more creative, and letting her ideas live.

Frederica has every right to be proud. It is a profound achievement when students overcome their own fears, risk failure, and come to believe, as Jeff Sturges noted, that they have "the power to make change both in their own lives and in the world around them."

Building on the concepts of persistence and learning from failure, another general thinking disposition associated with stuff making was craftsmanship. David Clifford defined craftsmanship as "doing something with care and doing something like you care. Doing something in the process of practicing patience, resilience, perseverance, and being able to do something because you want to do it well." Whereas the passion, patience, and persistence involved in Duckworth's definition of grit are present in David's definition of craftsmanship, doing something with care, doing something like you care, and doing something because you want to do it well introduce an element of quality and integrity to the work of young makers.

David's definition of craftsmanship is resonant with how longtime educator, builder, and carpenter Ron Berger has described what it means to be a craftsman—and the importance of having craftsmanship cross over to the classroom:

> In carpentry there is no higher compliment builders give to each other than this: That guy is a craftsman. The one word says it all. It connotes someone who has integrity and knowledge, who is dedicated to his work and who is proud of what he does and who he is. Someone who thinks carefully and does things well.

I want a classroom full of craftsmen. I want students whose work is strong and accurate and beautiful. Students who are proud of what they do, proud of how they respect both themselves and others.[21]

Beyond persistence, developing a sense of craftsmanship indeed means developing certain skills but also entails developing a sense of high standards to which to hold oneself. Attention to detail and having pride in one's work are all hallmarks of the variety of craftsmanship—and character building—that is supported by maker-centered learning experiences.

Many of the educators and thought leaders we spoke with associated community making as an important student outcome. More specifically, they highlighted perspective taking and empathy as being foundational to the character building that takes place in the maker-centered classroom. In particular, Gever Tulley spoke of developing the ability to see the world from other people's perspectives by discussing the project ideas that young people work on at Brightworks as windows on the world. "Any one of these little ideas is really a sort of keyhole to the rest of the world, and by looking at it through that keyhole, through that perspective, we see things we thought we understood before in new ways," he said.

So that's the point—to make sure that kids are questioning their own assumptions about the world and the things they think they know, and by seeing it from these other perspectives they learn more about themselves and more about the world, their place in it, and the ways they can change it.

Another maker educator we spoke with who emphasized the importance of perspective taking was Susie Wise. At the d.school at Stanford University, Susie is the director of the REDlab, where she teaches and studies maker-centered learning through the lens of design thinking. Susie discussed the empathy building and perspective taking work she does with young people in terms of need finding. Speaking from the perspective of her students, Susie said, "So it's not just 'Can I come up with an idea,' but it's actually need finding. 'Can I connect to other people and understand their needs and use that as the engine for what I might create?' It's trying to get to a deeper understanding of another person's perspective in order to come up with something new."

Beyond just seeing the world from other people's perspectives, the educators we spoke with also believe it is important for students to develop empathy—the ability to understand, identify with, and experience the feelings of others. David Clifford's example of students reflecting on their assumptions about homeless individuals exemplifies the need for reaching out and understanding others. Empathy as a necessary character building skill in the maker-centered classroom connects with the design thinking concept of human-centered design. IDEO, a design firm well known for popularizing design thinking, characterizes human-centered design as being "all about building a deep empathy with the people you're designing for,"[22] emphasizing the importance of identifying with the end user of product design. But Susie, David, and Gever's articulation of empathy as a character-building skill supported by maker-centered learning was far more global, and far more personal, than taking the needs and interests of "users" into account. Whereas design thinking concerns itself with users, the empathy that develops through maker-centered learning is more concerned with the needs, interests, and feelings of one's own community members. Here, a community can be understood as something as local as the members of one's classroom or as global as the residents of an entire city, state, or region.

Understanding the Secondary Outcomes of Maker-Centered Learning: Cultivating Discipline-Specific and Maker-Specific Knowledge and Skills

In addition to the disposition-based outcomes of agency and character, the participants in our study identified two sets of maker-centered learning outcomes that have less to do with supporting students as they develop a new way of seeing themselves in the world and more to do with providing students with new knowledge and skills (Figure 1.4). These capacity-based outcomes include cultivating *discipline-specific knowledge and skills* and cultivating *maker-specific knowledge and skills*. The educators we spoke with viewed these capacity-based outcomes as important but as secondary to the disposition-based outcomes discussed above. Cultivating discipline-specific knowledge and skills and maker-specific knowledge and skills, however, does not occur separately from cultivating the disposition-based outcomes discussed previously; rather, the participants in our study viewed these capacity-based outcomes as being instrumental to developing agency and character.

Cultivating Discipline-Specific Knowledge and Skills

In a maker-centered learning experience that focuses on complex circuitry, it might not be surprising that scientific, technological, and engineering knowledge and skills may be seen as core learning outcomes. The maker educators we spoke with acknowledged that they wanted students to develop just such discipline-specific knowledge and skills. However, they almost always framed these outcomes as being instrumental to achieving the disposition-based outcomes of agency and character. For instance, a teacher may emphasize the importance of understanding how individual electronic components can be connected by conductive wires, but the goal of understanding circuitry would be to empower students to use that knowledge in the maker-centered classroom to take on any number of challenges.

Consistent with the educational narrative in the popular press, the maker educators we spoke with did mention the STEM subjects when they discussed the skills they had hoped their students would learn. Indeed, many of the individuals worked in specific environments where teaching one or all of the STEM subjects was a primary goal. But even in these settings, equipping young people with STEM knowledge and skills was never an end unto itself, but rather was a means to achieve broader student-centered outcomes. Even Karen Wilkinson noted that what she and her staff at the Exploratorium, which is a science museum, really cared about was the "competence building, that empowerment, feeling like you're capable and confident about approaching things."

Although it is not surprising that Karen's work in a science museum connects specifically to STEM content, many of the other educators we spoke with did not work in STEM-oriented environments but still talked about the value of equipping young people with the knowledge and skills associated with these subjects areas. Like Karen, they viewed students' learning in these areas as instrumental to greater goals. "We're not trying to train engineers and technologists and things like that," commented Jeremy Boyle, codirector of the Children's Innovation Project in Pittsburgh, Pennsylvania. "Sure, there will be some children that go down that path, but what we really hope to do is support habits of mind." Steve Teeri, founder of the HYPE Teen Center at the Detroit Public Library in Detroit, Michigan, likewise noted the instrumental nature of cultivating discipline-based knowledge and skills.

Photo by Agency *by* Design

FIGURE 1.4: Students at the Corrales Community Library in New Mexico work with educators from the Parachute Factory to explore the properties of electricity using circuits, conductive thread, and LED lights.

"I am not actively rooting for any of the teens to become an engineer or computer programmer," he said. "If they do, that's wonderful. My goal here is to just aid them in becoming better people and better able to interact with the world around them, and when they go on to whatever it is they go on to I hope that we have helped them become better people in doing that."

In addition to cultivating knowledge and skills in the STEM subjects, many educators also highlighted the importance of developing knowledge and skills in other disciplines, such as English, history, and the arts. They noted that these disciplines could be taught through a maker lens, and they identified knowledge and skills associated with these domains as being potential outcomes of the work they engaged in.

Cultivating Maker-Specific Knowledge and Skills

In addition to acquiring discipline-specific knowledge and skills associated with particular topics and disciplines, these educators also wanted students to develop knowledge and skills associated with specific tools and technologies (Figure 1.5). For example, in a cabinet-building class in which students are encouraged to experiment with different joinery techniques, young people might venture to make their own hand-cut dovetail joints. Through that process, proficiency with the use of bevel-edged chisels and a dovetail saw would be important learning objectives. And indeed, our educators talked about wanting young people to understand how tools work, when they should be used, and how they could be used to the greatest effect.

This points to a second dimension of the maker-specific knowledge and skills mentioned by the participants in our study. Beyond proficiency with tools, techniques, and technologies, they also spoke about maker-specific practices as important outcomes of this work—practices such as prototyping, iteration, and tinkering. Though these practices take place in many other learning environments (e.g., writing multiple drafts of an essay in the English language arts classroom, conducting multiple experiments in the science classroom, sketching multiple drafts of an image in the visual arts classroom), participants identified prototyping, iteration, and tinkering as cornerstone practices of maker-centered learning. Similarly, they talked about the development of entrepreneurial skills as a specifically maker-centered practice.

FIGURE 1.5: A student at King Middle School in Portland, Maine, carefully chooses from a selection of chisels, making sure she uses the right tool for her wind turbine project.

To be sure, entrepreneurial skills are relevant to other areas as well. However, selling ideas and inventions to other people is often a part of a maker experience, and several of our educators talked about developing a business plan, an elevator pitch, or a social media strategy as part of the skill set associated with maker-centered entrepreneurialism.

Recapping the Real Benefits of Maker-Centered Learning

It has been incredibly illuminating for us to learn from our colleagues what they see as the *real* benefits of maker-centered learning. As enlightening as this experience has been, it has also been a challenging one. By asking educators and thought leaders to describe what they viewed as the benefits of maker-centered learning, we were essentially asking our colleagues to articulate concepts there may not necessarily be language yet to describe. As we dug deeper into the analysis of our interview data, we quickly came to understand that to communicate our findings we had to tentatively offer new ways of describing the concepts that emerged. The particular names and labels we have given the various outcomes described in this chapter are decidedly tentative. At the very least, what they aim to communicate is that the outcomes of maker-centered learning, as perceived by educators and thought leaders who are deeply immersed in the field, are far more nuanced—and arguably more interesting—than the dominant narratives commonly offered by the mainstream media.

To recap, the pursuit of the question, How do maker-centered educators and leaders in the field think about the benefits and outcomes of maker-centered learning experiences? has yielded a primary and a secondary set of student outcomes (Table 1.1). We found that the participants in our study identified the development of agency and the building of character to be the primary outcomes of maker-centered learning. Based on the way they discussed these outcomes, character and agency can be understood as dispositions that are deeply related to one another, with character building serving as a support for the can-do spirit that empowers young people to see themselves as agents of change in the world.

In the maker-centered classroom, developing student agency can be understood in terms of stuff making and community making. Building character can be understood as a form of self making, which involves building competence, building confidence, and ultimately forming an identity as a maker. For students, these two primary outcomes—developing agency and building character—are integrated in the maker-centered classroom through a focus on developing a variety of general thinking dispositions. Some of these general thinking dispositions are best described in terms of stuff making (e.g., risk taking, persistence, learning from failure, and craftsmanship), whereas others may be best described in terms of community making (e.g., perspective taking and empathy).

TABLE 1.1: The primary and secondary benefits associated with maker-centered learning

Primary Benefits of Maker-Centered Learning	
Developing Student Agency	
Stuff Making	Finding opportunities to make things that are meaningful to oneself and taking ownership over that process of making.
Community Making	Finding opportunities to make things that are meaningful to one's community and taking ownership of that process of making, either independently or with others.
Building Character	
Self Making	Building competence as a maker, building confidence in one's maker abilities, forming a maker identity.
General Thinking Dispositions	Supporting various patterns of thinking that are perceived as being beneficial across domains.
Secondary Benefits of Maker-Centered Learning	
Cultivating Discipline Specific Knowledge and Skills	
Fostering the development of knowledge and skills within the STEM subjects and other disciplines.	
Cultivating Maker Specific Knowledge and Skills	
Fostering the development of knowledge and skills with regard to maker-specific tools and technologies.	
Fostering the development of knowledge and skills with regard to maker-specific processes and practices.	

The secondary outcomes of maker-centered learning are more capacity-based in nature. They include discipline-specific knowledge and skills, such as those involved in STEM and other school subjects, and maker-specific knowledge and skills related to tools, technologies, and practices. Though the educators who were interviewed clearly value these capacity-based outcomes, they almost always spoke of them as being instrumental to the more disposition-based outcomes of developing student agency and building character.

Outcomes are simply ideals until they are connected to actual practices that turn them into reality. Accordingly, the next chapter addresses the second core question of our study: What are some of the key characteristics of the educational environments and instructional designs under which maker-centered learning thrives?

Teaching and Learning in the Maker-Centered Classroom

Chapter One considered how educators think about the benefits and outcomes of maker-centered learning. In contrast with the arguments focused on science, technology, engineering, and mathematics (STEM) and economics often heard in the popular press, we offered an alternative narrative about the real benefits of maker-centered learning experiences that have to do with helping young people develop a sense of agency and build character. In this chapter we further explore how maker educators structure their teaching and learning experiences by addressing the second core question of this book: What are some of the key characteristics of the educational environments and instructional designs under which maker-centered learning thrives?

Continuing to draw from our interviews and site visits, we address this question in four parts. The first part asks the question, Who (and what) are the teachers in the maker-centered classroom? The answer may seem obvious: They are people like the educators we interviewed. Well, yes, but it turns out there is a lot more to the story. The second part asks the question, What does teaching look like in the maker-centered classroom? Here we discuss the instructional moves and strategies that maker educators emphasize most often when they talk about their teaching practice. The third part asks the same question from the perspective of students: What does learning look like in the maker-centered classroom? In many ways the answer to this question is the flip side to the previous question: Students learn what they are being taught. However, as this section illustrates, our conversations with educators revealed a more nuanced story. Finally, the fourth part asks, What does the maker-centered classroom look like? Here we explore the various decisions educators make when they design their maker-centered classrooms to make them work for students, achieve their learning goals, and give them their distinctive feel. While each of these four questions will be explored in detail in the pages ahead, Table 2.1 provides an overview of the key characteristics that support maker-centered learning, as they were discussed by the educators and thought leaders we spoke with.

TABLE 2.1: Overview of strategies for designing maker-centered learning experiences and environments

Who (and What) Are the Teachers in the Maker-Centered Classroom?	
Students as Teachers	Students function as teachers in a variety of ways, including teaching one another, teaching the teacher, and teaching others in the school community and beyond.
Teachers in the Community	Community members often serve as resources for students in the maker-centered classroom, offering onsite and offsite expertise and mentorship.
Online Knowledge-Sourcing	Students access the Internet to find information and instruction.
Tools and Materials as Teachers	Students are encouraged to learn from the their physical interactions with tools and materials.
What Does Teaching Look Like in the Maker-Centered Classroom?	
Facilitating Student Collaboration	Teachers structure assignments and projects to encourage students to work together in a variety of formal and informal ways, and provide ongoing support for them to do so.
Encouraging Co-inspiration	Teachers design instruction so that students are encouraged to engage with and derive inspiration from one another's work.
Encouraging Co-critique	Teachers provide strategies and support for students to give each other informative, useful, and generous feedback.
Redirecting Authority	Teachers actively redirect students away from the fallback of "teacher as the authoritative dispenser of knowledge" and toward other authorities, especially other students and online resources.

(continued)

TABLE 2.1 (CONTINUED)

Who (and What) Are the Teachers in the Maker-Centered Classroom?	
Promoting an Ethics of Knowledge Sharing	Teachers take a "learn something, teach something" approach to encourage students to feel a sense of responsibility to share their newly developing skills and knowledge with others, especially other students in the maker-centered classroom.
What Does Learning Look Like in the Maker-Centered Classroom?	
All of the Above	Students learn by engaging in the various activities teachers encourage, including collaboration, co-inspiration, co-critique, seeking skills and knowledge on their own, and sharing skills and knowledge with others.
Figuring It Out	The most pervasively visible sign of student learning in the maker-centered classroom is students trying to figure things out on their own, especially through tinkering and iterative processes.
What Does the Maker-Centered Classroom Look Like?	
Tools and Materials	Maker-centered classrooms incorporate tools and materials from multiple disciplines.
Storage and Visibility	Tools, materials, and student work need to be stored within the maker-centered classroom. The more visible tools, materials, and student work are, the more likely it is that students will make new connections.
Specific and Flexible Spaces	Maker-centered classrooms tend to be either activity specific, or flexibly designed for engagement in a variety of maker-centered activities.

As with the outcomes discussed in the previous chapter, many of the maker-centered practices we discuss in these four sections are practices that have their roots in broader themes in educational theory and practice. So to set the stage, we begin this chapter with a brief overview of some of these major themes.

Maker-Centered Roots and Connections

Education professionals reading this book will rightly notice that many of the themes at the heart of maker-centered teaching and learning are not new. The themes of self-directed learning, of figuring things out on one's own, of learning by doing, of peer collaboration, are mainstays of progressive education. Here, with the foregoing discussion about signs of maker-centered teaching and learning in mind, we review some of the educational roots of these themes.

Perhaps the most fundamental relevancy is the work of the philosopher John Dewey. Across all of his many writings, Dewey emphasized learning by doing, an approach that has come to be known as a hands-on or an experiential approach to learning. Dewey rejected traditional notions of education that treated knowledge as a static commodity, capable of being deposited into passive minds as one might deposit money into a bank account. Rather, he viewed knowledge-making as a dynamic process that unfolds through reflective, iterative interaction with the practical demands and challenges of *doing* things.[1] He is oft-quoted: "Give the pupils something to do, not something to learn; and the doing is of such a nature as to demand thinking, or the intentional noting of connections; learning naturally results."[2] If John Dewey were to walk into any of the maker-centered classrooms we visited, he would easily recognize learning in action as he watched students tinker and experiment, iterate and fail, and reflect on their practical experiences to inform their next steps (Figure 2.1).

Two educational theories that build on Dewey's ideas and connect directly to maker-centered learning are *constructivism* and *constructionism*. Jean Piaget, the Swiss psychologist often considered the father of constructivism, argued that knowledge is constructed via the interaction between learners' conceptual schema, or frameworks, and their experiences in the world to which those schema are applied.[3] Considered through a maker lens, Piaget's theories connect to maker-centered learning's strong emphasis on tinkering and figuring things out, both of which involve starting with one's own ideas and then shaping those ideas based on direct, experiential action.

Constructionism, a view developed by mathematician and educator Seymour Papert, holds that learning happens best when learners work directly with manipulable media—from LEGO bricks to computer code—to build things that are sharable with others. Papert worked with Piaget early in his career, and he explained the relationship between constructivism and constructionism this way:

> *Constructionism . . . shares contructivism's view of learning as "building knowledge structures" through progressive internalization of actions . . . It then adds the idea that this happens especially felicitously in a context where the learner is consciously engaged in constructing a public entity, whether it's a sand castle on the beach or a theory of the universe.*[4]

FIGURE 2.1: Two young makers support each other as they learn about tools and materials.

Another area of educational theory worth considering as a backdrop to maker-centered learning is the work on peer learning. The findings described in this chapter underscore the social nature of maker-centered learning, and draw attention to the distributed nature of teaching and learning in the maker-centered classroom. Much of the literature on peer learning can be traced back to the work of Lev Vygotsky, a psychologist widely known for promoting the idea that all learning is social. Vygotsky's concept of the zone of proximal development is particularly apt to the variety of peer learning that takes place in the maker-centered classroom. In his own words, Vygotsky described the zone of proximal development as

> *The distance between the actual development level as determined by independent problem solving and the level of potential development as determined through problem solving under adult guidance or in collaboration with more capable peers.*[5]

In maker-centered learning environments, students and educators fluidly function as both learners and teachers, often upending the traditional model of teacher-student relationship. One of the ways this plays out is that students are often teaching one another. Peer learning is by no means a novel idea in education, and much has been written about it. Broadly, peer learning has to do with students learning from and with each other. The benefits cited for peer learning usually include increased student self-esteem, teamwork, and perspective taking.

There are many varieties of peer learning: Cooperative learning is considered a form of peer learning because students are exploring ideas together. Peer tutoring is a form of peer learning because students are providing one another with direct instruction. Project-based learning is considered a form of peer learning because students work together to create something new. A form of peer learning discussed less frequently in the literature but very present in maker-centered learning is peer critique, which involves students learning from one another by providing each other with informative feedback. Also less discussed in the literature is the on the fly, ad hoc peer learning that is characteristic of maker-centered learning. This refers to the just-in-time knowledge sourcing that students are constantly doing for one another—for example, helping each other locate information, trying new things, and learning new skills. What is distinctive about the peer learning in maker settings is that it embraces all forms of peer learning. Not surprisingly, peer learning further connects strongly to the benefits of agency discussed in the previous chapter. As many of the maker educators we spoke with discussed, looking to one's peers as a source of learning rather than just to the teacher is a profound way of taking charge of one's own learning.

It is important to note that maker educators do not view peer learning simply as a nicety, something to be tacked onto instruction as an afterthought. It is part of the DNA of maker settings, where it is often necessary—either because students genuinely know things that their teachers do not or because the efficient distribution of skill-instruction requires it, such as when a large class of students needs to learn how to use a drill press and the fastest way to disseminate the information is for students to teach other students.

A final educational approach with significant connections to maker-centered learning is project-based learning (PBL), an approach to curricular design that organizes learning and teaching around projects. In a sense, project-based learning is the most obvious connection to maker-centered learning because making things is often synonymous with pursuing a project. There are indeed lots of similarities between the two approaches, but there are important differences as well. It is worth taking a close look at how the two approaches compare.

In project-based learning, the projects students do are typically pursued over an extended time period and revolve around a substantive inquiry question closely connected to curricular content. In a review of project-based learning theory in the *Cambridge Handbook of the Learning Sciences*, scholars Joseph Krajcik and Phyllis Blumenfeld describe project-based learning experiences as having the following characteristics:

1. They start with a driving question, a problem to be solved.

2. Students explore the driving question by participating in authentic, situated inquiry—processes of problem solving that are central to expert performance in the discipline. As students explore the driving question, they learn and apply important ideas in the discipline.

3. Students, teachers, and community members engage in collaborative activities to find solutions to the driving question. This mirrors the complex social situation of expert problem solving.

4. While engaged in the inquiry process, students are scaffolded with learning technologies that help them participate in activities normally beyond their ability.

5. Students create a set of tangible products that address the driving question. These are shared artifacts, publicly accessible external representations of the class's learning.[6]

Clearly, many of these characteristics can be present in the work of maker-centered learning as well. For instance, maker-centered learning is usually interest driven; it sometimes involves using expert knowledge and skills; it is frequently collaborative; it often involves the use of learning technologies ranging from paper-and-pencil concept maps to a variety of digital resources; and by making things, students do indeed create tangible products that are external representations of their learning.

But the differences between project-based learning and maker-centered learning are worth noting. Not all maker-centered learning experiences exemplify all of these characteristics. For instance, sometimes making begins with tinkering so that the inquiry questions are emergent and arise out of students' ongoing interactions with materials. Education researchers Sylvia Libow Martinez and Gary Stager define tinkering as "a mindset—a playful way to approach and solve problems through direct experience, experimentation, and discovery."[7] A further difference between maker-centered learning and project-based learning is that maker-centered learning often draws on disciplinary knowledge but doesn't always emphasize the importance of developing expertise. Instead, maker-centered learning tends to favor a just-in-time accessing of skills and knowledge when such skills and knowledge are needed. Yet another difference between the two educational approaches is that project-based learning is a well-worked-out instructional approach with a set of criteria, like the ones already cited, which are often used to frame an entire curriculum. Sometimes that is the case with maker-centered learning, but usually not. Instead, making weaves in and out of various classes and contexts, often having a designated conceptual and physical space of its own. Yet another difference is the nature of the inquiry questions that drives projects. Project-based learning pursuits are typically driven by broad conceptual questions that invite interdisciplinary inquiry. Sometimes this is the case with maker-centered learning, but sometimes maker-centered learning is driven simply by the lure and challenge of making cool stuff, like marble chutes or video games or wearable electronics.

In sum, maker-centered learning clearly has deep roots in the progressive learning theories of thinkers like John Dewey, Jean Piaget, Seymour Papert, and Lev Vygotsky. It is also clearly connected to educational approaches like peer learning and project-based learning. But despite these roots and connections, maker-centered learning has its own center of gravity, which is characterized by the themes mentioned in this and the foregoing chapter—themes like fostering student agency and building character, distributed teaching and learning, a celebration of tinkering and figuring-out behavior, and an ethics of knowledge sharing. In the chapter ahead, we explore these themes, beginning with an exploration of who—and what—are the teachers in the maker-centered classroom.

Who (and What) Are the Teachers in the Maker-Centered Classroom?

This isn't your typical classroom. I'm not necessarily your teacher. I'm not up here with all the answers.

—Mariano Ullibari

One of the most distinctive characteristics of maker-centered learning is that its teachers are anywhere and everywhere. Naturally, this includes the maker educator who happens to be in the room—the person students would point to as the teacher. But interestingly, when maker educators themselves talk about the teaching that occurs in their classrooms, they are likely to point to teachers beyond themselves.

Students as Teachers

The first source of teachers our educators pointed to were the students themselves. Every person we spoke with was convinced of the importance of encouraging students to teach, and to teach in a variety of ways. For example, sometimes students function as experts and straightforwardly teach skills and information they happen to know a lot about, such as how to use iMovie or create a *Minecraft* video. Their students in these cases are sometimes their fellow students, but they are also teachers, parents, and other adults in the community. Sometimes students teach skills they have just recently learned to other students who are right behind them in an arc of learning, such as how to load vinyl onto a vinyl cutter or how to change drill bits or unjam a sewing machine. Frequently students teach by serving as mentors to other students, offering guidance, coaching, feedback, and other kinds of skill- and confidence-building support.

Based on our conversations with maker educators, we found that the pedagogical roles students assume are just as varied as the roles the regular classroom teacher assumes, including teacher as dispenser of information, teacher as facilitator, teacher as connector, and so on. Later in this chapter we look closely at the various forms of pedagogy at play in maker-centered learning environments. For now, the important point is that students have a robust pedagogical presence, teaching in various roles and serving various constituencies. Maker educators explicitly encourage this, and in fact, as a group, the educators we talked with were twice as likely to point to students as teachers as all other types of teachers combined, including themselves.

This extreme emphasis on students as teachers is rare. It is even more unusual if one considers the context: Quite often in maker-centered classrooms, students are using complex machinery, working with tricky materials, and making things to be used in real-life and sometimes high-stakes contexts. Such a scenario would seem to favor a more traditional pedagogical model in which students are taught "properly" the first time, usually by the teacher or other expert in the front of the room. But almost the opposite is true. So what is going on? Why are maker educators so adamant about encouraging students to be teachers?

We heard three reasons. The first is the simple fact that sometimes students really are the experts. They know something that no one else in the classroom does, so it simply makes sense to ask them to teach it, as shown in Figure 2.2. Moreover, some maker educators aim to create student experts, precisely so they can teach. For instance, at Fox Meadow Elementary School in Scarsdale, New York, principal Duncan Wilson explained, "As long as every kid can get the basic experience we want them to have, then let them be the experts. I already have 3-D printing experts among the students. We're going to have soldering experts. We'll have Arduino experts."

A second reason maker educators encourage students to be teachers has to do with efficiency: having students play the role of teacher expands what maker educators can do in the classroom. One way this happens is by avoiding the bottleneck of teachers being the sole dispensers of information. As Peter McKenna, a technology teacher at Fox Meadow Elementary School, said, "If you try to teach 24 kids how to sew at once, you have a disaster on your hands." Peter's strategy is to teach three kids to sew on the first day and then to ask those students to teach the next group.

FIGURE 2.2: At the Open Bench Project, a makerspace in Portland, Maine, teachers come in all shapes and sizes. Brought in as a local expert, 13-year-old Aidan is seen here facilitating an Arduino class for King Middle School science and math teachers.

We heard many stories about this kind of tiered teaching, particularly in relation to learning skills like sewing and learning about various tools, like how to use a jigsaw. Indeed, many educators explicitly structure a tiered teaching sequence into their regular instruction. As Andy Forest of MakerKids in Toronto, Ontario, explained, "Frequently if I'm showing a group of kids how to use something like a jigsaw, and there's four people listed on the board that need to know how to use the jigsaw and one kid knows already, then I'll say, 'You teach it.' I fill in the gaps and make sure they covered everything—but it really makes them own the skill if they can pass it along to someone else."

In addition to relieving learning bottlenecks, having students teach also frees up the regular classroom teacher to play other roles. For example, reflecting on his time at the Opal school in Portland, Oregon, Steve Davee remembered the benefits of having students teach other students to allow him to assume the role of documentarian: "It allows me to go around and document, because here I am taking pictures, showing students that I'm looking at things, asking questions, hearing from them what they're doing, listening to them, and writing down quotes." Playing the role of documentarian is an important part of the educational surround, but it is one that often gets squeezed out when teachers put themselves in the position of being the sole classroom provider of direct instruction. At the Marymount School in New York, Jaymes Dec has been training his students to teach for a similar reason. "Now," he said, "we've got two or three student experts on each of the tools or machines or techniques we use in this lab. So students are teaching each other." The value of students teaching other students, he explained, is that "it frees up a lot of my time to be able to walk around and speak to the students and try to get them to expose what they're thinking about, and talk about their projects."

The third reason maker educators encourage students to be teachers is because it directly serves the educational goals and outcomes we described in the previous chapter. Andy Forest offered, "Kids teaching kids is really powerful for confidence-building. They're excited to teach other kids; it really makes them own the skill, if they can pass it on to someone else." In fact, Andy values kids teaching kids so much that he envisions a double-badge system, in which a student gets one badge for knowing a skill, and a second badge for teaching it.[8]

Steve Teeri, founder of the HYPE Teen Center at the Detroit Public Library in Detroit, Michigan, likewise stresses the value of young people teaching the skills and expertise they have gained to others. "When visitors come in unexpectedly and want to know about the makerspace, Terence is pushing us out of the way to explain all of these things we do here," he explained.[9] "Terence is one of the teens who is a regular at our workshops. We frequently find that when we're exhibiting at an event in the community and we have brought some of the teens like Terence with us, they are really excited to share what they have learned. Not only have they gained new skills, but they have gained confidence and a sense of accomplishment that they want to share." This theme, of helping students develop a sense of confidence and agency through teaching others was quite dear to many of the maker educators we spoke with, and we return to it several times throughout this chapter.

Teachers in the Community

Encouraging students to be teachers in the maker-centered classroom is a peda-gogical mainstay of maker-centered learning. But the sourcing of teachers also goes further afield. Students often do projects that require expertise beyond the walls of the classroom, and maker educators strongly encourage students to connect with experts in the local community who can teach them what they need to know (Figure 2.3). For example, in Portland, Maine, Gus Goodwin's students at King Middle School needed to learn how to mix fiberglass. Portland is a coastal city with an active seaport, so Gus helped his students connect with a local boat builder who could teach them the craft. At the Brightworks School, one of Gever Tulley's stu-dents was doing a project that involved making a complex map, so she was encour-aged to work with folks at a local tech start-up that specializes in mapping software. At the Mount Elliott MakerSpace in Detroit, Michigan, a group of students wanted to learn how to screen print T-shirts, so Jeff Sturges helped them connect with a mentor in the community who could teach them not just the craft of screen printing but also the entrepreneurial aspect of it.

Photo by Melissa Rivard.

FIGURE 2.3: Students work with a guest educator on a collaborative wind turbine project.

The walls of the maker-centered classroom are porous. Students easily pass beyond them to learn from members of the community, and the porosity goes both ways—members of the community are often invited into maker-centered classrooms to share their knowledge and inspire students. For example, we heard stories of visiting bike fabricators, Egyptologists, machinists, and farmers, all of whom have come to maker-centered classrooms to share their stories and teach their craft. We learned about tinkerers-in-residence, visiting inventors, and visiting artists who set up shop in maker-centered classrooms, sometimes to teach specific skills but sometimes simply to tinker and invent in the presence of young people, thereby teaching by modeling various versions of what it looks like to be a maker.

Online Knowledge Sourcing

Yet another source of instruction that maker educators embrace is not a person at all—it is the world of online information. The Internet is a huge teaching resource that offers an array of instructional experiences—students regularly go online to access text-based information, to watch demonstration videos, to get advice from other people, to explore and sometimes participate in professional communities related to their areas of interest, and to poke around and get inspired by seeing cool stuff. Online resources are a rich source of instruction that can be accessed in a variety of ways. Some of these resources, such as Instructables and DIY.org, are specifically designed for projects and maker-centered learning. But there are infinitely more resources that students can access simply by surfing the Web. We refer to online knowledge sourcing as a teacher because the educators we spoke with clearly view it as an important, and often crucial, teaching resource. As Duncan Wilson pointed out, "We have Chromebooks in fifth grade. That completely changes where the information comes from in the classroom."

Online knowledge sourcing is important not only because of the vast informational content of the Internet but also because finding information online usually requires a measure of self-directed learning. Students make choices about what paths to follow, they make judgments about the validity and reliability of information, and they review and recalibrate their learning as they go along. For these reasons, sourcing information online is often a form of agentic behavior, and thus connects to the goal of helping students develop a sense of agency.

Tools and Materials as Teachers

And ultimately we're trying to get them to listen to the screw.

—*Gever Tulley*

Maker-centered learning often involves working with tangible materials, and maker educators often talk about tools and materials as teachers (Figure 2.4). They want their students to listen and engage with materials, to respond to them, to get to know them deeply, to have conversations with them. The relationship is not just about learning specific techniques; it is also about extending the imagination. At East Bay School for Boys, David Clifford talked about students' use of tools as "touching points for making sense of the world." He elaborated, "Touching a tool and knowing what the tool does, using that tool and seeing what it does, are ways to understand possibility." Relatedly, Jeremy Boyle, codirector of the Children's Innovation Project, spoke about the ways in which tools and technology function like vehicles for making and learning—just like materials do. "The idea that technology is a raw material is something that is such an important part of our

FIGURE 2.4: In the Tech Ed room at King Middle School, tools and materials are ready for making and tinkering opportunities.

practice," he said, "because if we think about technology as no different from paint on a page, or clay being sculpted—technology becomes just something else you can make stuff out of."

At the Exploratorium's Tinkering Studio in San Francisco, Karen Wilkinson wants students to learn to be tinkerers by learning to converse with materials. "If you have developed a tinkerer's disposition," she said, "you have this way of asking questions of cardboard . . . responding to its feedback, trying something else, and having a dialogue with a material or an idea."

It is noteworthy that maker educators think about the way materials and tools function as teachers in the same dialogical way as they view their own teaching—as a reciprocal relationship that is characterized by conversation and feedback and encouragement rather than by the direct transmission of skill. Speaking again of listening to the screw, Gever Tulley said:

> There is multisensory feedback in driving a screw; it goes zuck and the screwdriver stops, each of the senses working together to provide that positive feedback. You see that the first time they get it to happen, because the screw is talking directly to them in a nuanced way that we can never match as external observers. Ultimately we're trying to get them to build that relationship with their work all the time.

Zooming back to the question, Who (and what) are the teachers in the maker-centered classroom?, the answer is that the role of teacher is distributed and variable. It is distributed in the sense that the function of teaching is distributed across multiple agents. These agents include the classroom teacher, members of the wider community, various online portals, physical tools and materials, and, very importantly, students themselves. The role of the teacher is variable because these agents play their teaching roles in various ways, including providing direct instruction, giving how-to advice, modeling behaviors, functioning as a coach or a mentor, and playing the role of documentarian. This variability in modes of teaching is noteworthy, particularly in terms of understanding the role of the lead maker educator—the person students would point to as the classroom teacher, if asked—and it brings us to the question of how maker educators themselves characterize the teaching they do.

What Does Teaching Look Like in the Maker-Centered Classroom?

So making, at some level, leads to teachers having to really ask themselves questions about their own instructional tolerance levels, because making is messy. It's noisy. It all doesn't happen on the same schedule. And you can't assess it with a multiple choice test.

—*Pamela R. Moran*

In her role as superintendent of Albemarle County Public Schools in Albemarle, Virginia, Pam Moran sees a lot of teaching in action. As her words above suggest, teaching in a maker-centered classroom presents challenges and opportunities that are unlike those that educators may experience in other learning environments. That being said, there are also plenty of commonalities. In any setting, most educators who teach young people are likely to play several different roles. At times they are a traditional didact, standing up in front of a class and dispensing information. Sometimes they function as a facilitator, bringing students together and facilitating interactions between them. Sometimes they function as a coach, encouraging students to persist and excel. Sometimes they teach by modeling desirable behavior or by adopting a mentor role. Sometimes they function as a counselor, tending to students' social and emotional needs. Sometimes they even teach by admitting they are not the bearers of all knowledge and by learning right alongside their students. The capacity to flexibly teach in different ways is a common characteristic of good teaching in general, so it is not surprising that maker educators, like good teachers everywhere, play multiple pedagogical roles. However, what we wanted to better understand from the maker educators we spoke with was what roles they emphasized when they talked about their teaching. In other words, what do maker educators think is important about their pedagogical approach?

Hopefully by now it is clear that maker educators are an inventive bunch. Their pedagogical techniques are numerous and cannot easily be classified. In the maker spirit, they employ whatever teaching roles and methods happen to suit their purposes at the moment, responding and adapting to students' needs as they go along.

Nonetheless, as we sifted through our interview transcripts, we noticed an underlying purpose that seemed to unify most of their pedagogical moves and intentions: to teach in a way that enables self-directed, interest-driven, peer-involved learning. To support this goal, they tended to mention three broad areas of teaching activities most often: facilitating student collaboration, encouraging co-critique and co-inspiration, and redirecting authority.

Facilitating Student Collaboration

Walk into a maker classroom and you are likely to see clusters of students working together, as shown in Figure 2.5. Collaborative learning is a familiar term in education, and it refers to a wide range of practices, from highly structured cooperative learning groups to informal peer feedback. Not surprisingly, maker educators seem to have a broad and expansive conception of collaboration. In their view, it is a hallmark characteristic of maker classrooms, and it occurs in a variety of ways. For instance, often in the maker-centered classroom students collaborate on projects in which they make things or tackle a design challenge together. Sometimes students collaborate by finding and sharing resources, even if they are working independently. They often collaborate by teaching one another, as described in the foregoing section. Sometimes they collaborate by giving one another feedback, or by simply giving each other a hand with whatever is needed.

Given the pervasiveness of collaboration in the maker-centered classroom, it makes sense that when maker educators describe what they do when they teach, they view supporting student collaboration as a crucial part of their role. Some of the support they provide students is simply typical orchestration and management—for example, getting students into groups, helping them find time to work together, and providing goals and guidelines for group projects. Other times, they create highly structured collaborative experiences for students—and other times collaborative learning happens all on its own.

In the world of education there are many other ideas about what the term *collaborative learning* means and about the frameworks to structure collaborative learning experiences.[10] As noted earlier in the discussion of peer learning, there are also different forms of and reasons for collaboration. For example, collaboration can

Photo by Melissa Rivard.

FIGURE 2.5: A third grade student asks a friend for help as she explores the properties and stretching capacity of a new material.

refer to any kind of informally shared group work, or teamwork, or to highly structured cooperative experiences where each group member shares equally in the work.

Closely related to educational views about collaborative learning is educational theory about the processes of group invention and innovation—collaborative processes that often take place in the maker-centered classroom. Here theorists have made the case that not only is learning distributed, but so, too, is the variety of creativity that takes place in the maker-centered classroom.[11] From the perspective of distributed creativity, various young people participate in the development of ideas in much the same way that the educators we spoke with described the collaboration that takes place in their maker-centered classrooms. As mentioned earlier, students *participate* in making through a do-it-together process that involves the engagement of multiple individuals. With this in mind, some maker educators have connected the variety of distributed invention that takes place in the maker-centered classroom to the concept of *participatory culture,* which is often used to describe engagement and learning through digital media.[12]

Themes of collaboration, participation, and distributed invention may seem at odds with a cultural movement that has been branded as a do-it-yourself (DIY) renaissance, but as David Lang has pointed out in his book *Zero to Maker*, no one ever really makes anything on their own.[13] DIY is a misnomer. Making and maker-centered learning are instead about doing things together, or, as Lang puts it, the maker movement is a do-it-together (DIT) revolution.[14]

Indeed, the maker educators we spoke with embraced the do-it-together nature of their work with young people, and they frequently used the term collaboration to describe the various manifestations of DIT in their learning environments. They did not, however, seem particularly concerned about defining collaboration narrowly. In fact, many educators viewed the collaborative spirit as an expression of the mutual encouragement and support that is part of the zeitgeist of the maker-centered classroom. As Steve Davee put it, collaboration "becomes this collective group effort that is a beautiful sign of what happens when you take a bunch of makers and put them all together in a room and say, 'Alright, how do you support each other? What can emerge by this mutual support?'"

Maker educators do not, however, gloss over the fact that collaboration often comes along with arguing and negotiation. In fact they will often create conditions where these characteristics arise in ways that can get worked out naturally. For example, Steve Davee talked about setting up situations where there are limited resources—say, a handful of Hot Wheels cars and some half-gutters on a small hill on the playground—and then letting a group of kids go at it. With a little gentle attention from him on the sidelines, Steve watched students move from "fighting over something limited to cooperating over something limited." His goal in these situations was not so much for students to learn how to efficiently "get things done" but rather to help them develop a sense of care and responsibility toward one another. He talks about how the set-up of limited physical materials helps students face and deal with an issue, like ". . . how do you share, how do you not covet that particular car, how do you make sure somebody is included?"

From within this frame of care and responsibility, maker educators naturally also emphasize the practical benefits of collaboration. They want their students to understand that projects are genuinely better when people work together in ways that include different voices, different talents, and different skill sets. As Gever Tulley stressed, he wants his students to understand that even when things are complicated, "they can find the right partners and suddenly the juices start flowing, and then things become possible and they can do it."

In the current educational climate, collaboration is often talked about as a 21st century skill—something students will need to master if they are to be successful in the contemporary world. Indeed, the influential Partnership for 21st Century Learning framework (P21) identifies collaboration as a key educational outcome, and defines it as the ability to "work effectively with diverse teams, and be helpful and make necessary compromises to accomplish a common goal."[15] The maker educators we spoke with would probably agree with this as far as it goes. But it is important to keep in mind the real benefits of maker-centered learning discussed in Chapter One. Beyond the mainstream media narrative that stresses the potential impact of making on the national and global economy, the educators we spoke with stressed the importance of developing student agency and building character through maker-centered learning. To the extent that they would agree with P21's definition of collaboration, they would likely do so from the standpoint of care and character development rather than workplace-oriented efficiency. What this means in practice is that maker educators facilitate collaboration by doing such things as listening closely to each student and trying to understand individual needs; organizing group projects so that they represent social, intellectual, and academic diversity; designing project tasks and presentations so that they surface the voices of underheard students; and paying careful attention to the social and emotional dimensions of group dynamics (Figure 2.6). They do all of this while continually emphasizing the power of working together.

Encouraging Co-inspiration and Co-critique

As the previous section makes clear, facilitating student collaboration is an important part of what maker educators do. Often this involves a direct focus on student collaborative groups. But even beyond structured collaborations, maker educators

FIGURE 2.6: Lighthouse Community Charter School teacher Amy Dobras facilitates a Grade 7-8 collaborative making project exploring identity, self-worth, and community.

find ways to help students learn from and with one another. The maker educators we spoke with discussed the process of learning from and with one another in two distinct ways, which can best be described as *co-inspiration* and *co-critique*. Co-inspiration involves creating opportunities for students to explicitly borrow and build on each other's ideas. Co-critique involves creating opportunities for students to give each other informative, generous, and productive feedback. Both instructional practices involve teaching students to look closely at the specific features of their peers' work and to translate their observations into words or actions.

Co-inspiration

Gus Goodwin has a teaching technique he calls *making the rounds*. He uses it when students are making something together in small groups. It goes like this: Once students begin to settle into their work, Gus instructs one student from each group to go around the room and look at the other groups' projects and sketch what she sees at each table. She returns to her group, at which point one of her other team members leaves to observe and sketch another group. The process continues until everyone has had a chance to observe and sketch other groups' work. At the end of the rounds, the members of the group compare what they saw, discuss what inspired them, and decide how they want to modify and improve their project going forward. Gus's intention is to get students to look closely at each other's work and use one another as sources of inspiration.

Rather than "stealing" ideas from one another, this process of co-inspiration can be seen as a form of collegial appropriation (Figure 2.7). As the education scholar Edith K. Ackermann described, "Appropriation is the process by which a person or group becomes acquainted with, and gains interest in, things by making them their own. It is an eminently creative process, often resulting in unexpected uses, clever détournements, and surprising outcomes."[16]

FIGURE 2.7: After "making the rounds" and observing other groups' wind turbines, students in Gus Goodwin's technology education class discuss ways to incorporate what they have learned into their own model.

Over at the Exploratorium's Tinkering Studio, Karen Wilkinson is also a believer in this objective, and she gets excited when she talks about how young people's ideas can be contagious. As an example, she tells the story of how one girl in the Young Makers Club at the Exploratorium built a tree house for fairies. It had a clever little pumping fountain and lots of appealing lights. What was really cool about it, Karen explained, was its verticality, the way it was built along a wall. She was not the only one who thought it was cool. The space in the Tinkering Studio is designed for co-inspiration, and the fairy house was displayed in a way that encouraged other students to easily examine it. As it turned out, its various innovative features inspired several other students' designs. Karen enthusiastically described how the inspiration was "literally kid to kid. It wasn't anything we were instructing."

Karen may not have been explicitly telling students to inspire one another, but she and her colleagues at the Exploratorium have certainly put a lot of thought into how the physical features of a space can tacitly support co-inspiration. She noted that even the shape of a worktable can make a huge difference, and told a story of when the Tinkering Studio first began its open make series. At the time, the space was furnished with rectangular tables for people to work at. During one of the open make events, a staff photographer happened to take a picture of the tables in use from above. Karen and her colleagues came to call the scene an "angry buffet" because it looked like everyone was crowding in to get a glimpse of what the person at the head of the table—usually the instructor—was doing. After experimenting with different table arrangements and sizes, they eventually discovered that round tables worked the best (Figure 2.8). Physically speaking, a round table precludes anyone from assuming the head. With the teacher-at-the-front-of-the-room mentally ingrained in most of us, it is hard not to solely look to the head of the table for inspiration, thereby missing much of what other people are doing. Round tables, Karen found, work much better to help spread kid-to-kid ideas.

Co-critique

Teaching techniques for supporting peer-to-peer inspiration are often closely related to techniques for supporting peer-to-peer feedback, or co-critique. This is

FIGURE 2.8: In its original configuration, the Tinkering Studio in San Francisco's Exploratorium offered rectangular tables for visitors to make things. After observing an unintended teacher-at-the-head-of-the-table mentality, staff refurnished the space with round tables, thereby increasing the potential for distributed learning and teaching.

Photo by Agency *by* Design.

because both practices involve getting students to look closely and carefully at one another's work from the standpoint of a generous, probing, productive mindset. Many educators view co-critique as an important part of the learning process. Among them are Ron Berger, a veteran teacher and carpenter who has long encouraged teachers to make critique a habit of mind that young people apply across their school experiences. From Berger's perspective, peer-to-peer critique is a form of learning that doubly benefits students by helping them become more sensitive to design and by driving their work forward. Berger's approach to critique is simple. He encourages students to be kind, be specific, and be useful.[17]

Similar to Berger's approach to structuring peer-to-peer critique, the maker educators we spoke with likewise shared a variety of strategies they used. In the Tinkering Studio, Karen favors the strategy of "plussing," a technique popularized by the animation studio, Pixar. The cardinal rule of plussing is that you cannot offer a criticism unless you also offer a positive suggestion. Like Karen, Pixar adopted the technique to counter people's natural tendency to see obstacles rather than solutions. Without a co-critique strategy like plussing, offbeat ideas that might grow into something great tend to get shot down before they even get off the ground.

Across the country in Maine, Gus Goodwin explains that he is always experimenting with various ways to encourage productive peer feedback among his students, and that he often switches things up. For example, one strategy he uses directly leverages the power of close observation. He will put one group's project on a table and direct the entire class to look closely at it. He tells them to ask questions, and notice features, but to withhold judgmental comments, even if the judgments are positive, like "looks good." Instead, he wants them to make specific observations, like noticing the use of a gear for a certain function, or the unusual use of materials. At other times, Gus encourages peer feedback by pairing students up and giving them a graphic organizer that explicitly walks them through a process of productive co-critique that includes noticing details, noticing positives, and suggesting improvements.

An important part of supporting productive co-critique is giving students a clear lens through which to think about feedback (Figure 2.9). Susie Wise told us that when her students from the REDlab at Stanford University's d.school are engaged in a design project, she encourages co-critique from the perspective of the end user of the design under development. To do this, Susie has her students share their projects with one another and listen carefully to try to understand the intended audience behind a design; then, they examine each other's projects closely and try to vividly imagine how the design will work for the person or group it is intended for. What works well? Where are the potential sticking points? How can it be improved? By having students take the perspective of the end user, Susie makes sure that the emphasis of the critique is squarely on making a project better, rather than simply pointing out its flaws.

FIGURE 2.9: At Brightworks School in San Francisco, California, students' self-designed studio spaces include specific areas for sharing ideas and soliciting feedback. Here, a student seeks design advice from a friend.

Whatever their strategies, maker educators share the basic goal of teaching productive co-critique, which means creating experiences in which students can give and receive genuinely useful feedback—feedback that is thoughtfully informative rather than unthinkingly judgmental. Obviously this goal is not unique to maker-centered learning. Plenty of teachers in all kinds of settings encourage their students to be inspired by one another's work, and to give each other thoughtful feedback. What is distinctive about maker-centered learning is that co-inspiration and co-critique play such a prominent role. Indeed, they are outward expressions of a fundamental philosophy of teaching, described next, that was shared by virtually all of the maker educators we have met.

Redirecting Authority and the Ethics of Knowledge Sharing

As every educator knows, teaching happens tacitly as well as explicitly. Teachers teach not only with words but also with the messages they send through the expectations, values, and norms reflected in the everyday culture of their classrooms. Distilled to its simplest formulation, the central idea behind teaching is to help learners acquire knowledge. Accordingly, much of the tacit messaging of instruction communicates fundamental ideas about knowledge—what it is, where it comes from, who has it, and what behaviors and responsibilities are attached to it. It is here, in what might be called the epistemology of maker-centered learning, that we find one of the root ideas that inform maker-centered teaching. It is the idea that knowledge can be accessed from many sources in the maker-centered classroom, most especially from the students themselves, and that maker-centered learning offers the opportunity, and responsibility, to take part in a system of knowledge-sharing.

Through our visits to various maker-centered classrooms and our conversations with maker educators, one of the instructional practices we heard about over and over again was some version of a strategy for redirecting students away from the fallback idea of the teacher as the sole and authoritative dispenser of knowledge (Figure 2.10). Jeremy Boyle, codirector of the Children's Innovation Project, spoke directly about this:

> As teachers we need to simultaneously engage as learners, and make that transparent. We like the idea that students ask lots of questions that we can't answer. And as teachers we have to accept that we don't know all of the answers. Instead, we need to engage in the process of exploring the answers to interesting questions together with our students. So the teacher becomes the facilitator of that process. And that's key.

Photo by Melissa Rivard.

FIGURE 2.10: In Ed Crandall's ninth-grade robotics class students look to each other for technological help and advice.

Jeremy makes an important point, but he also raises an important and interesting question: If teachers are not necessarily the authorities in the maker-centered classroom, then who is?

At the Mt. Elliott Makerspace in Detroit, Michigan, one approach to redirecting authority that Jeff Sturges favors is called the rule of five. When students ask him a question about how to do something, whenever possible he redirects them by saying, "Ask five people and average the answers, or bother somebody five times before they say, 'Leave me alone.'" Jeff wants students to understand that with knowledge comes responsibility. When they have knowledge that others can use— knowledge of a skill, a procedure, a set of facts—they are responsible for teaching it. He is very clear about this with his students. "It is a very specific thing I say to them," he explained. "If I teach you something, you've got to teach someone else."

This knowledge-sharing ethic translates directly into his teaching practice. "Because I'm sort of the leadership figure," he said, "students are always coming to me, and I'm like, 'Ask him. Ask somebody else. Ask the Internet. Ask me last. There are many different ways to find things out,'" he tells his students, "Google it, ask your friends, Google it many different ways, ask five different people."

Many of the educators we spoke with practice some version of this technique. In Andy Forest's classroom in Toronto, there is a running list on the blackboard. Andy explained, "Students put their name on the board when they need to learn a skill. If students see something up on the board that they know how to do, then we'll get them to teach it to the other kids in the class. We try to encourage them to help each other as much as possible, and recognize that as a valuable endeavor."

Steve Davee also emphasized the values dimension of knowledge sharing. "Learn a skill, teach a skill," he would tell his students at the Opal School, and he views the redirecting of teaching authority as one of his key roles as an educator. Steve describes how he watches students closely, looking for a tone of voice or a body movement that shows a student is getting just good enough at a skill so that she is ready to share it with someone else. Then, when another student comes to him with a particular need, he redirects them to the student he has been observing. Steve sees himself as a conductor and a matchmaker, and he is clear that in playing these roles his aim is to explicitly communicate an ethics of knowledge sharing. What he wants students to understand, he explained, is that teaching others is "really a responsibility you take for yourself when you learn something."

Not surprisingly, this strong emphasis on knowledge sharing resonates with the larger ethos of the maker movement. The resonance has to do with a belief in the value of sharing skills and ideas, a celebration of just-in-time learning, a focus on process, and a joyful participation in the maker community in which knowledge and skills are freely exchanged.

This section began with the question, What does teaching and learning look like in the maker-centered classroom? Drawing extensively on our conversations with educators, as well as site visits to various maker-centered classrooms, we have highlighted some of the characteristic instructional moves that educators tell us they make, along with the beliefs and ideas that animate those moves. There are surely important features of maker-centered instruction we have not discussed. But we feel confident reporting that, at the very least, the three broad features we have described are of concern to most of the educators we spoke with: (1) facilitating student collaboration whenever possible and in a variety of ways; (2) encouraging co-inspiration and co-critique among students, and (3) promoting an ethics of knowledge sharing by redirecting students' quest for authoritative knowledge away from the classroom teacher and toward other sources of inspiration and information, most especially the other students in the room.

What Does Learning Look Like in the Maker-Centered Classroom?

Suppose you are a principal in a school with a robust maker program. Your school has a busy makerspace in a room adjoining the cafeteria, and at any hour of the day it is occupied by groups of students working on various types of projects. Additionally, many teachers in the school, inspired by students' enthusiasm for making, are integrating maker-centered learning activities into their classes. The district superintendent has been supportive from afar, and one day she arrives at the school and wants to see firsthand what all of the buzz is about. You show her the makerspace, but you also make sure to talk with her about the real outcomes of maker-centered learning, beyond the snazzy projects on display. You point out that yes, the projects are impressive, but what is really impressive is the sense of agency students are developing, their sense of confidence and competence, and their sense of identity as makers. The superintendent listens appreciatively, and is eager to see for herself. "Why don't I walk around and take a look in some classrooms," she says. Then she pauses. "Tell me," she adds, "what exactly should I be looking for?"

The superintendent asks a good question. She wants to know how to recognize the signs of maker-centered learning in action. To a large extent, teaching and learning are two sides of a coin and the answer to her question mirrors the dimensions of maker-centered teaching discussed in the section above. For example, as the superintendent tours the school, she is likely to see lots of examples of distributed teaching and learning—she may see students teaching students, students teaching teachers,

teachers and students learning alongside one another, and students knowledge-sourcing from one another and online. She might see some community members working with students in the classroom, or maybe the empty desks of students who are working with community members outside of school. She is also likely to see lots of collaborative activity among students, from students working together on projects to helping each other find resources to offering one anther feedback. There is also something else she can look for, if she really wants to see the essence of maker-centered learning in action—students figuring things out for themselves.

Figuring It Out

If there is a hallmark activity of maker-centered learning, it is the process of trying to figure things out. It could be trying to figure out different ways of creating a ramp for a marble to roll down, or how to write code for digital animation. It could be figuring out how to take a toy apart, how to make a circuit, or how to build a model bridge that withstands simulated seismic quakes. The specific behavior students engage in to figure these kinds of things out varies. It might involve wiggling around parts and manipulating materials, or accessing information online. It might be finding someone who knows how to do something you want to do and getting them to teach you. It might involve cycles of trial and error, of iterating and prototyping, or simply the process of locating a set of instructions and following them step by step. The common theme across all of these varieties of figuring-out behavior is that each one involves choice and ongoing self-direction as the process plays itself out. Students who figure things out make choices about what they will do and try to find a solution, and then they use feedback from their efforts to inform their next set of choices. In this way, they are exercising agency in support of their own learning.

One mode of figuring-it-out behavior that maker educators are especially fond of is tinkering. Gever Tulley, founder of the Brightworks School and the Tinkering School summer camps, says that tinkering often begins when someone has a model of something that gets them started, but they know it is not right yet. So they play around with materials and experiment with different approaches until they arrive at what they want (Figure 2.11).

FIGURE 2.11: Staff at the Tinkering Studio model their own philosophy by experimenting with exhibition designs.

Tinkering is a form of figuring-out behavior, but it has its own emergent, often meandering character. In their beautiful book about makers and their products and processes, *The Art of Tinkering*, Karen Wilkinson and Mike Petrich of the Exploratorium talk about tinkering like this:

> *It's more of a perspective than a vocation. It's fooling around directly with phenomena, tools, and materials. It's thinking with your hands and learning through doing. It's slowing down and getting curious about mechanics and mysteries of the everyday stuff around you. It's whimsical, enjoyable, fraught with dead ends, frustrating, and ultimately about inquiry.*[18]

Maker educator Jaymes Dec of the Marymount School of New York juxtaposes tinkering to step-wise design thinking or problem-solving processes and believes that it sometimes best characterizes the work of scientists. "Talk to scientists, and they don't follow this scientific method the way it's taught in school," he said. "It's a much more sort of tinkering and just trying things out approach. And a lot of the type of stuff that I'm trying to encourage kids to be comfortable doing is the type of stuff that scientists do, where they'll just try something out and see if it works." Jaymes sees making as a "tinkering, exploratory, bricolage approach" and worries that overlaying a prescribed, step-wise problem-solving process onto maker-centered learning undercuts the excitement and whimsy of it.

So back to you and the superintendent. You have talked to her about the signs of maker-centered learning in action, and she begins her tour. What will she be looking for? For starters, she may look for students clustering in various configurations, sometimes working closely together on a project, sometimes showing each other how to do things, sometimes giving each other feedback and advice. She may look for teachers learning alongside students, and sometimes from students as well. She may also look for signs of students figuring things out on their own, often by tinkering with materials and processes. She may hear students saying, "Let's try this," or "look at what happened when we did it this way," or "maybe we should do it this way instead." She may look for playfulness and experimentation, for persistence and iteration. She may listen for students voicing their own ideas, and watch for signs of them making their own choices about how to work through a challenge. This means, of course, that she may see lots of what is commonly called failure and problem solving—experiments and efforts that yield not their hoped-for results but informative feedback about how to keep on keeping on.

The superintendent knows that taken individually, each feature of maker-centered learning can be seen in other educational settings. Hopefully, what she will come to see as she tours your school is that maker-centered learning is an energizing context in which many of these features coalesce to add up to far more than the sum of their parts.

In addition to observing student behavior, as the superintendent tours your school she is also likely to notice that specific choices have been made about the physical spaces where maker-centered learning takes place. The following section discusses the environmental characteristics of various maker-centered classrooms, based on our site visits and discussions with maker educators in many of these unique and exciting spaces.

What Does the Maker-Centered Classroom Look Like?

In addition to having its own philosophical center of gravity, maker-centered learning can be understood as having a distinctive physical center of gravity as well. Often drawing on the premise of the environment as a *third teacher*,[19] a fundamental component in the preschools of Reggio Emilia, Italy, many maker educators have offered advice for how to set up maker-centered learning environments, and many books have been published on this topic. Among them are Rachelle Doorley's *Tinkerlab*, which offers useful hints on how to turn one's home into a tinkering studio for little inventors; Laura Fleming's *Worlds of Making*, which builds on her experiences establishing a library-based makerspace for New Millford High School in New Millford, New Jersey; and Scott Doorley and Scott Withhoft's popular *Make Space*, which offers tips from the Stanford d.school for setting up an environment conducive to creative collaboration.[20]

Though the maker-centered classroom can take many forms, through our interviews and site visits we came to understand that maker-centered learning often occurs in special settings—makerspaces, fablabs, tinkering studios—and its placeness is a strong contributing factor to what makes maker-centered learning feel so unique (Figure 2.12). Within these spaces, educators make careful decisions about how to set up an environment that is most conducive to their learning goals.

FIGURE 2.12: The Innovation Workshop at Park Day School was built after many conversations, surveys, and meetings involving school and broader community constituents.

Although there is no one way to outfit and arrange a maker-centered classroom, we discuss several consistent trends—and tensions—that emerged from our study.

Tools and Materials

In his book *The Maker Manifesto*, Techshop CEO Mark Hatch includes "Tool Up" as one of his nine core tenets of the maker call to action.[21] Indeed, considering what tools to have on hand in the maker-centered classroom is an important decision. In fact, one of the most popular questions we are asked by educators interested in bringing maker-centered learning to their schools or communities is, *What kinds of tools should I get for my makerspace?* Hatch takes the answer to this question very seriously. In his book, he devotes over two pages to listing out the essential tools necessary to support a maker revolution.[22] Among them are extravagant pieces of equipment such as plasma cutters, sandblasting cabinets, powder coating systems, and a 4′ x 8′ CNC waterjet cutter. While we applaud the thoroughness of Hatch's tooling up list, we have come to find that powerful maker-centered learning experiences can take place in much more modestly equipped settings, with much simpler tools.

During a visit to the Innovation Lab—or I-Lab as they call it—at the Nueva School in Hillsborough, California, Kim Saxe, the director of the school's I-Lab and design thinking program, suggested to us that some of the most modest tools and materials are the most important ones. The Nueva School's I-Lab was designed in collaboration with students and faculty from Stanford University's d.school, and it includes some of the high-tech manufacturing equipment that appears in Hatch's

Photo by Melissa Rivard.

FIGURE 2.13: Students working at Park Day School frequently use simple tools, like glue guns, to prototype their ideas with non-precious materials.

tool up list. Nonetheless, during our visit Kim told us that a glue gun and some cardboard are often the most effective tools and materials in the space (Figure 2.13). What Kim suggested is that using simple tools to fix together inexpensive materials is often the quickest way for students to develop prototypes of their ideas—and that a great deal of learning takes place through the iterative process of down and dirty prototyping.

Similarly, during an early visit to Lick-Wilmerding High School in San Francisco, California, faculty from the Technical Arts department likewise downplayed the necessity of tools and equipment that are frequently associated with maker-centered learning. Lick-Wilmerding High School, founded as an Industrial Arts school in 1894, has a long tradition of training young people in woodworking, fabrication, electronics, and design. As a result, the technical arts classrooms look like clean, well-outfitted and maintained, professional workshops. And while the Lick Wilmerding technical arts faculty likewise have many of the gadgets associated with maker-centered learning, they are careful not to overemphasize them. "A 3-D printer is the sixth most important tool in a makerspace," one of their faculty members told us during our visit, suggesting that although 3-D printers have their place, students can learn much more about making and fabrication by working with more traditional tools and materials.

Many of the educators we spoke with stressed that good work can be done with basic tools, but we also found that some of the educators we spoke with emphasized the importance of providing young people with access to high-quality equipment. During a visit to East Bay School for Boys, David Clifford proudly handed us the screw guns and drills in his school's workshop, which he said were the best that money could buy. David firmly believes not only that young people should have access to authentic tools and equipment but also that those tools and equipment should be of the very best quality. Working with high-quality tools not only shows respect for the young people who use them, but also supports the development of craftsmanship and the pursuit of quality work.

Storage and Visibility

Another popular topic discussed in many of the maker-centered classrooms that we visited was the importance of storage and visibility. When it comes to maker-centered learning, there are lots of things that need to be stored, including materials, tools and equipment, and student work. During a visit to the Bright-works School, school director Ellen Hathaway gave us a tour of the space, pointing out the importance of having materials on hand for whatever sort of project might pop up. One of Ellen's suggestions was to never throw away materials from past projects but instead to always keep old materials on hand because one never knows when they might be needed again. But holding on to so much stuff means that there must be space to put it. Ellen went so far as to suggest that a maker-centered classroom should have just as much storage space as work space. The Brightworks School has done an impressive job of holding on to stuff, without having the place feel cluttered and overcrowded.

In the maker-centered classroom, how things are stored has an effect on how accessible those things are to students. During our visits to Mt. Elliott Makerspace, Marymount School of New York, MakerKids, and many other spaces, bins of gadgets and materials were both well-labeled and reachable by even young students. Jeff Sturges and others emphasized the importance of keeping as many tools and materials in view and at the ready at all times. Jeff's philosophy is that the visibility of tools and materials in a maker-centered classroom sparks ideas and helps students make connections that they may not have made otherwise.

Conversely, across town at the HYPE Teen Center in the Detroit Public Library, Steve Teeri keeps all his maker tools and supplies in a large walk-in storage space, and just pulls out the tools and materials students need at a particular time. During our visit to the HYPE Teen Center, Steve described how this process works. "We have a former meeting room/study room which has been converted into our storage space," he said. "We have racks of shelving and we have Sterilite plastic storage bins. We just keep all of our equipment and materials there, and we just pull out whatever we need to use for that two-hour workshop, do it over the course of two hours, put everything away, and put it back into the storage space."

The HYPE Teen Center is a 4,000-square-foot space that is centrally located right next to the main entrance of the Detroit Public Library. The makerspace is just one component of the larger, multiuse space. Steve described how storing tools and materials in the way that he does is necessary to better integrate maker-centered learning into the greater work of the Teen Center—and to promote visibility on a whole other level:

> The reason we store our tools and materials is that we don't want to have the makerspace be in its own room in the basement or on the second floor of the library away from the Teen Center where people would not see the activities going on. So in this way we don't have a dedicated space, which we could have had if we really wanted to, we have a lot of space in this building, but instead maker activities take place in the existing Teen Center without totally taking over the Teen Center.

Having just the tools and materials necessary for a particular project helps students focus—and it also helped Steve manage his tools and materials in a public space that receives lots of traffic (Figure 2.14).

Photo by Melissa Rivard.

FIGURE 2.14: In many makerspaces, visibility of materials, tools, and projects in process are critical to how kids engage with the making and tinkering process.

Relatedly, another important trend we noticed during our various site visits was that frequently used tools and materials all had their place. Scanning through photographs we took reveals image after image of hand tools hung neatly on walls, often outlined in black Sharpie; transparent plastic bins of materials neatly arranged and clearly labeled; and other careful arrangements of clamps, screw guns, and chisels. Though maker-centered learning can frequently be messy work, sharing the responsibility of caring for equipment and establishing a system for storing frequently used tools and materials is a key component of maintaining a sense of order—and knowing where your tools are—in the maker-centered classroom.

Specific and Flexible Spaces

Yet another trend we noticed during our site visits to various maker-centered classrooms was the designated use of space as either being specified for a particular purpose, or purposefully flexible by design. Clear examples of specified spaces can be seen at King Middle School, the East Bay School for Boys, and the Athenian School's maker barn. At each site, a clean space directly adjoins a messier workspace. In the clean space students frequently sketch out ideas, perhaps using paper and pencil or by working on computers; in the messy space, students work with large-scale tools and materials. Here, messy is not exactly the right word, because the workshop spaces at all of these sites are frequently cleaned, but they are indeed spaces where sparks fly and sawdust builds up while students are at work. This is not to suggest that no making happens within the clean space. At the Athenian School's maker barn, for example, the 3-D printers and laser cutters are kept inside the clean space, and frequently materials that are cut or welded in the messy space are then assembled in the clean space. But the feel of each is certainly different. One obvious distinction between the two spaces is the necessity to wear safety goggles in the messy space—which are not required in the clean space.

Though not having the same clean space/messy space divisions, many other maker-centered classrooms we visited had specific spaces designed for specific purposes. At Lick-Wilmerding High School, certain workshop spaces were designated for woodworking or metal working, and other spaces were designated for electronics or jewelry making. The tools of each of these spaces matched their designated purposes.

Though many maker-centered classrooms we visited compartmentalized their workspaces based on the types of tools present in different workshops or separated the clean and the messy aspects of making from one another, other spaces combined everything in one flexible space intentionally designed to be constantly redesigned. One example of a flexible space is the Brightworks School. While the school certainly has designated areas for working with different tools and materials, the majority of the space is composed of simply framed structures that can be taken apart and rebuilt over and over again, based on students' current work demands. Students at Brightworks are given agency to design their own studios, which are referred to as treehouses—partially because many of them incorporate actual logs and tree branches and partially because they are often two-story structures that provide students with a bird's-eye view of their learning environment.

Earlier in this chapter we mentioned that we are often asked by educators and administrators eager to bring maker-centered learning to their schools and communities the question, What tools do I need to have in my makerspace? Based on our conversations with maker educators and our site visits to various maker-centered learning environments, we have come to understand that, contrary to Hatch's Tool Up list, there is no single set of essential tools that are used in the maker-centered classroom. Tools, technologies, and materials ought to be aligned with the thinking and learning goals in the classroom; in other words, the physical space and materials should support the maker-centered learning objectives—not the other way around. In fact, we often respond to the question, *What tools do I need to have in my makerspace?*, by suggesting that the most important tool to have in a maker-centered classroom—and the place from which to start—is a framework for thinking and learning. In later chapters we offer one possible framework when we turn to addressing the third guiding question of this book, What kinds of educational interventions can support thoughtful reflection around maker-centered learning and the made dimensions of our world? But first, in the next chapter we discuss what the Agency *by* Design team has come to believe is one of the most important promises of maker-centered learning: providing an opportunity for all students to develop a sense of maker empowerment.

Developing a Sense of Maker Empowerment

Jimmy's got a backpack—and it's the coolest backpack ever. While his dad was on a business trip to Japan three years ago, he saw this backpack in the window of a sporting goods store, and he thought his son would like it. He was totally right. Jimmy loves his backpack. It's yellow and blue with white trim and tons of cool pockets. The shoulder straps fit just right, and there is even an extra strap that Jimmy can clip across his chest so that the pack doesn't wobble around when he is learning new tricks at the skate park with his friends. Inside there's a bunch of compartments for pens and stuff and a secret compartment for his phone with a cool silver grommet where his earbuds pop out. Jimmy's made the backpack even cooler. He's used paint markers to write the names of his favorite bands all over the outside and stenciled the logo of his favorite skateboard company across the back. But the coolest part was that while he was at the X Games in Austin launch last year, Jimmy got Nyjah Huston to sign his name in black Sharpie over the left side pocket. Dude, Nyjah Huston!

Even though it was starting to look a little worse for wear after three years of Jimmy toting it around every day, Jimmy's backpack was still perfect to him.

Until it wasn't.

A few weeks ago—the same day Jimmy landed his first fakie kickflip 180—the zipper broke. It wasn't just any zipper—the main zipper to the big compartment where Jimmy kept his books and stuff for school. Without the zipper, the bag flopped open and everything fell out.

This was a problem—a huge problem.

At first, Jimmy tried to repair the backpack with safety pins. A quick fix, just to keep the main compartment secured. The safety pins looked cool, kind of punk rock, but they were too weak to keep the backpack closed. They got all tweaked and bent out of shape from the weight of Jimmy's books. He couldn't even ollie onto a curb without his bag popping open—and it was such a pain to undo, like, a dozen twisted safety pins just to get his books out.

"Jimmy," his mom had said, "let me get you a new backpack."

Jimmy was grateful that his mom offered to buy him a new backpack, but that was totally not an option. There was no way he could go from having the coolest backpack in school to having a bag just like everyone else.

But the zipper problem was really getting out of control. A week passed. Jimmy was about to cave in and finally start looking for a new backpack. But then one day while he was skating home from school, the Sew Low fabric store caught his eye. Jimmy went in and started looking around. There were tons of brightly colored fabrics everywhere and a whole wall filled with different sorts of fasteners. Jimmy was a little overwhelmed, but he was on a mission. After a few minutes of roaming around, he went up to a woman behind a counter and showed her his backpack. "Do you think I can fix it?" he asked.

This was an important question. Jimmy didn't ask the woman in the fabric store, "Can you fix it?" He asked her if he could fix it. Of course, Jimmy already knew he could fix it, but he was mostly just asking how.

Jimmy's a maker. Every time Jimmy sees a new skate video down at the shop, he immediately heads out with a handful of friends to see what cool new street ramps they can build. They study the skate videos carefully and copy the ramps in the videos as best as they can. Sometimes they make perfect replicas that work awesome. Other times things don't work out so well—but they always wind up making some sort of structure that turns out to be just as cool.

Jimmy didn't know the first thing about how to fix a broken zipper, but the lady at the fabric store totally hooked him up. In no time Jimmy was on his way home with a bag full of sewing gear—and a brand-new zipper. He had what he needed to fix his backpack, now all he needed was to figure out how to do it. So he opened his laptop and hopped on YouTube. There were hundreds of videos showing how to replace a broken zipper. A few hours of YouTubing later, and after pricking his fingers like, a million times, he'd finally done it. He'd finally removed and replaced the zipper—and it totally worked!

Jimmy's new zipper wasn't perfect, and he had to tweak it a few times when the seams he'd sewn had started to give, but that didn't matter. What mattered was that Jimmy still had the coolest backpack in school, and now it was even cooler

The story of Jimmy is a story of empowerment. It speaks to one of the main goals of the Agency *by* Design research initiative, which has been to better understand what maker educators and thought leaders in the field viewed as the primary outcomes of their work. Through interviews and site visits, the Agency *by* Design research team quickly began to notice some themes. In one way or another, we consistently heard educators say that they were hoping for their students to develop a can-do spirit, or as Bruce Hamren at The Athenian School said, "a feeling like you have the ability to say, 'I can do that'—and then actually do it." Just like Jimmy.

Rather than being mere consumers of their worlds, Bruce and others want their students to develop as producers. For example, educators would point to a set of headphones, a backpack, or a chair and say they wanted their students to view these everyday objects not as commodities they could buy but as opportunities for them to invent, create, and innovate.

Initially, our understanding was that this can-do spirit applied to the many commodities young people have the opportunity to purchase in our consumerist culture. However, as we continued to listen to maker educators speak, we noticed that their interest in helping students develop the can-do spirit reached far beyond the making of objects. They wanted to encourage a mindset in their students—a way of seeing and being in the world—that extended their sense of I-can-do-that beyond objects to social, cultural, and political systems. As one example, David Clifford made the case that a young person's experiences making in school could potentially lead to students feeling empowered to challenge major cultural systems, such as our country's dominant paradigm of systemic racism.

As the Agency *by* Design team members synthesized what we were hearing during our early conversations with educators, we began to interpret the colloquial notion of I-can-do-that as agency. In fact, the name of our project, Agency *by* Design, derived from our early recognition that student agency is a core driver, and goal, of maker-centered learning (Figure 3.1). As Chapter One attests, educators in the maker sphere seem to care deeply about cultivating a sense of agency in their students—but not just any kind of agency. The educators we spoke with wanted their students to develop a sense of agency with regards to making (or remaking) things in the world. Sometimes those "things" were actually things—like furniture, smartphone cases, or wearable electronics. Other times those things were systems, like the major cultural forces David Clifford mentioned, but also like more localized systems such as the system for lining up for lunch at school or the system for doing chores in one's home. This chapter presents the notion of maker-centered agency as a disposition and offers the focal concept of maker empowerment as its core spirit. Maker empowerment is meant to describe student agency through a maker

Photo by Jeanine Harmon.

FIGURE 3.1: Students build confidence and competence when given an opportunity to work with carpentry tools.

lens. Shortly, we discuss this specific concept at length—offering a definition, and several examples. But first it may be helpful to say a few words about the more general concept of human agency.

What Is Agency?

People exercise their agency when they consciously choose to act in ways that are intended to bring about certain effects. This may sound straightforward, but its surface clarity masks a wide range of questions that have animated philosophical debates for centuries. Does our capacity to make choices about how we act mean that we have free will? Maybe, but maybe not. Philosophers have pointed out that it is possible to have the feeling that one is acting freely and by choice when in fact the machinery of the universe predetermines everything that happens. Is the faculty of agency the property of an individual mind? Maybe, but some sociologists would argue that our choice-making behaviors are so profoundly shaped by social and cultural systems that the idea of individual choice is an illusion.

Views about the nature of human agency are fundamental to our understanding of issues as diverse as the nature of intention and action, the possibility of free will and autonomy, issues of ethics and moral responsibility, explanations of rationality and *akrasia* (weakness of will), theories of human motivation, theories of economic behavior, and theories of human rights. Ideas about the meaning and purpose of human agency have been put forth by a wide range of scholars in a wide range of professions, including philosophers, psychologists, ethicists, theologians, neuroscientists, lawyers, sociologists, feminists, and human rights activists, to name just a few. It would take this chapter far afield to try to review the scholarly literature on agency. Instead, what we offer below is a brief subjective synthesis of selected conceptual aspects of human agency that have direct bearing on the concept of *maker empowerment*—the particular brand of agency we have identified as being the core outcome of maker-centered learning.

Choice, Intention, and Action

Many philosophers and psychologists believe that the capacity to have a sense of agency with regard to one's individual actions is one of the hallmark traits of human existence. At the most basic level, agency has to do with choice, intention, and action and can be defined as our species' capacity to make intentional choices about how to act in the world. This is a broad and somewhat anodyne definition that most theorists would agree with. But its simplicity is only surface deep. Poke at it a bit, and things immediately start to get complicated.

For starters, note that this loose definition of agency refers to the capacity to make choices about how to act, not just the capacity to act. Linking agency to choice narrows down the kinds of actions that can be agentic to actions that are both conscious and intentional. In other words, acting with a sense of agency means that you are aware of what you are doing—that you have an intention to act the way that you do and that you are aware that you could make a choice to act otherwise.

So, for example, an automatic action like withdrawing your hand from a hot stove does not count as agency. Nor does an action you make voluntarily but for which there is no real viable alternative, like obeying a judge when she tells you to pay a parking ticket. These are actions, but they lack conscious and freely given intention. In a way, both pulling one's hand away from a hot stove and paying a parking ticket can be understood as individual *reactions* to a stimulus on the level of immediate response. Pulling your hand from a hot stove is an immediate biological response; paying a parking ticket is an immediate sociocultural response. To do otherwise in either of these scenarios would suggest an agentic action, because there would be an intention to act in opposition to one's ordinary biological or sociocultural immediate responses.

Another complicated feature of the concept of agency has to do with the relationship between intention and action. Does having a sense of agency entail *taking* action—perhaps even successful action—to qualify as having a sense of agency? Not necessarily. For example, suppose you are an experienced cyclist and you have just gotten a flat tire. You know you can fix your bicycle tire yourself, and under certain conditions you would. But right now you are in too much of a hurry and have neither the tools you will need to fix your flat nor an extra tube. It is just faster to take it to a shop.

Oftentimes it is quicker to pay someone else to do something for us rather than to do that thing ourselves. In this scenario, you could wait to fix your flat yourself, but then you would not have access to your bicycle for several days. And that would not be practical. Taking your bicycle to the shop to get it fixed in a hurry may cost you a little more, but it solves the problem more quickly. Here you are not lacking a sense of agency; you are lacking the time, tools, and materials to act on that sense of agency.

This example highlights an important distinction: the difference between having a sense of agency and participating in agentic action. Or in other words, the difference between saying to yourself I can do that, and actually doing it. The psychologist Albert Bandura is widely known for his scholarship on agency and self-efficacy. In his work on these topics Bandura has argued that there are several "core properties of human agency."[1] Among these core properties is intentionality: "People set themselves goals and anticipate likely outcomes of prospective actions to guide and motivate their efforts."[2] But as Bandura notes, intentionality is not enough:

> *Having adopted an intention and an action plan, one cannot simply sit back and wait for the appropriate performances to appear. . . . Agency thus involves not only the deliberative ability to make choices and action plans, but also the ability to construct appropriate courses of action and to motivate and regulate their execution.*[3]

On one hand, having a sense of agency describes a tendency toward action rather than stipulating a strict requirement of action. Having a sense of agency is a potential state; the preparedness for future action. On the other hand, agentic action is a performative state that operationalizes these tendencies, and realizes one's potential to participate in agentic behavior. Maker empowerment emphasizes the potential state of having a sense of agency over the performative state of participating in agentic behavior. This emphasis on tendency-defined rather than rule-defined behavior turns out to be important when we discuss the concept of maker empowerment as having a sense of agency with regard to the made (and yet-to-be-made) dimensions of one's world.

Scope: Agency and the Complex Web of Interrelated Actions

Two additional features of the general concept of agency are useful to bring into focus and consider through a maker lens. The first feature is *scope*, which has to do with the grain-size of actions we want to refer to when we talk about having a sense of agency. Agentic choices can occur across a continuum of human action, from tiny choices we make thousands of times a day, like choosing to walk from point A to point B, to grand choices we make about which life paths to pursue and how to pursue them. The sense of agency reflected in the I-can-do-it spirit that maker educators we spoke with clearly goes beyond the agency of a single act. These educators were not referring to students' capacity to decide to pick up a hammer or order an Arduino online. Rather, they were referring to students' willingness to choose to engage in a prolonged and often complex web of interrelated actions.

Gever Tulley tells just such a story. Recently Ana,[4] a Brightworks student, had visited an underresourced school in one of San Francisco's neighborhoods. What she learned while she was there was that the school's library was woefully underequipped and that the students did not have access to books they could check out and take home to read at night. An avid reader and the daughter of an English teacher, Ana found this scenario unacceptable. She refused to live in a city where other young people her age did not have access to books—and she was inclined to do something about it.

"She literally was wondering if she could just empty our shelves and take them there," Tulley noted, "but instead we guided her into a 'think about this as a project or something you could do that would keep providing books to the school' mindset." And that's exactly what Ana did. After raising $1,200 and providing the school with over 700 books, Ana has now set up an initiative connecting local bookstores with the school so that unsold inventory with the covers removed can be channeled to the school's library.

Inspired by her experience at the Brightworks School, where students pursue self-directed projects on a regular basis, Ana had the wherewithal to take the steps she needed to change a flawed system. While she may not have built or made something in the traditional sense, Ana was nonetheless maker-empowered—seeing the world as malleable, alert to an opportunity to create change, and capable and inclined to do so.

Gever tells an elegant story of Ana's experiences, but in reality the amount of work, the number of choices, and the decisions Ana had to make throughout this process indicate that agentic behavior is multilayered, intricate, and complex. Indeed, Ana's experiences at Brightworks had equipped her with a general sense of agency, but moving beyond having a sense of agency toward agentic action required Ana to develop a fundraising campaign, to establish communications with various booksellers, to connect with school librarians, and to place a system into action that would later run on its own. Throughout this process, Ana wrote letters, sent emails, made phone calls, and appealed to a variety of people in person to persuade them to help her out. Although having a sense of agency entails having a tendency toward action, engaging in agentic behavior involves both the pursuit and the execution of a complex, multilayered web of interrelated actions.

Like the example of Ana, the actions that the educators we spoke with had in mind when they talked about maker-centered agency tended to encompass a large sweep of smaller choices, such as learning new skills, seeking out resources, and collaborating with others (Figure 3.2).

FIGURE 3.2: In a partnership between Emerson Elementary School and Park Day School, students build T-Stools to bring back for classroom use.

Photo by Jeanine Harmon.

Locus: Participating in Agentic Action

A second important feature of the concept of agency as it relates to making, designing, redesigning, and hacking is the locus of agency. The term *locus* refers to where a sense of agency originates and resides. As with scope, the spectrum of possibility is vast. At one extreme end is a fully internal view, in which a sense of agency originates wholly from the internal workings of an individual mind. At the other end is a fully external view, in which an individual's sense of agency is wholly socially constructed and arises solely through the influence of external environmental factors such as cultural expectations, social networks, and the material influences of the physical world. From the standpoint of common sense, situating agency at either of these extreme ends is implausible. On one hand, radical internalism doesn't make sense because none of us lives in a vacuum; our actions and decisions cannot help but be influenced by the people and places around us, at least to some degree. On the other hand, radical externalism is implausible because it would mean that any sense of interior mental control we have over our own choice-making is simply an illusion and that every agentic action we (mistakenly) believe we author ourselves is in reality determined by outside forces.

The wide middle between these two extremes leaves lots of room for the positioning of agency. Through our site visits, interviews, and work with teachers, we have come to believe that a maker sense of agency tilts clearly toward an external view, generously acknowledging the roles of culture, community, and the physical environment in shaping agentic behavior. Or as Bandura puts it, "Most human pursuits involve other participating agents, so there is no absolute agency. . . . Effective group performance is guided by collective intentionality."[5] The complex web of interrelated actions that Ana engaged in above also consisted of a complex web of interrelated individuals—bringing shape to the social nature of agency and making visible the collective nature of agentic action.

Bandura has referred to this concept as *collective agency*:

> *People do not live their lives in individual autonomy. Indeed, many of the outcomes they seek are achievable only through interdependent efforts. Hence,*

they have to work together to secure what they cannot accomplish on their own. Social cognitive theory extends the conception of human agency to collective agency. People's shared beliefs in their collective power to produce desired results are a key ingredient of collective agency.[6]

Though Bandura emphasizes the social nature of collective agency, he is keen to note that the individual does not get lost in the process. Rather, individuals assert their agency within collective efforts. This concept is emphasized in Brittany Harker Martin's framework for socially empowered learning. "When students are socially empowered," she argues, "they feel they can make a difference in their lives and the lives of others."[7] From the perspective of maker-centered learning and the broader ethos of the maker movement, it can be said that the individuals within broader communities of makers come together, each asserting their own individual agency, to achieve greater effects. Bandura's concept of collective agency dovetails nicely with the idea of do-it-together mentioned in Chapter Two. Reflecting on his own experiences of becoming a maker, David Lang has made this point very clearly: "Making is about sharing ideas, tools, and processes. The most prolific makers I met weren't the people who did everything themselves. In fact, they were the individuals most skilled at navigating the web of collaboration and adapting it to their will."[8]

As discussed in Chapters One and Two, maker culture tends to be highly collaborative, community based, and reliant on information sharing. Maker-centered activities are situated in flexible and often sprawling sociocultural networks, which include people, cultural forces, information, and materials that are operant in the immediate vicinity as well as people, resources, cultures, and information that are accessed digitally from a geographical distance. As such, when one asserts one's agency within a maker context, one is often *participating* with others.[9]

An example of collective agency that emanates from distributed maker participation can be found in the following vignette provided by Aaron Vanderwerff, director of the Creativity Lab at the Lighthouse Community Charter School in Oakland, California:

"Convert a gasoline truck to electric power—for real? We thought you were joking!"

And with that it was on—Roberto, Cesar, and Tomas would spend much of their extra time in the spring of their senior year working to convert a twenty-year-old truck from gasoline to electric power as the final project for their Making elective.[10] Along the way they learned to weld, read circuit diagrams, and machine parts for the truck. But those weren't the most important benefits of taking on this project.

Early on the young men needed to find money to pay for the project. So together, they applied for a grant through our local utility company and were funded. Then the guys scoured Craigslist for a truck that would be ideal for a conversion. They called innumerable strangers, dealt with the idiosyncrasies of used automobile sales, and eventually bought a vehicle and got it to the school parking lot. They borrowed an engine hoist to remove the engine, found a conversion kit, learned to collaborate with their mentors, and called electric vehicle (EV) conversion companies for technical information. If you've ever worked with high school students, you know how hard it can be to get them to make a call to a stranger, but these guys were on fire.

The pinnacle of their journey was when they drove from Oakland to Sebastopol—a small town culturally a world away. There they got help from an EV enthusiast to machine their own adapter plate, the part that would connect their new electric motor to the existing transmission. At that point, I knew the boys were onto something special.

Through this project Roberto, Cesar, and Tomas were empowered to do things they would not have dreamed of doing previously. Tomas was even talking about opening up his own conversion business after graduation.

The most amazing thing was the effect this empowerment had beyond their making elective class. Two of these young men were in danger of not graduating. Their writing wasn't strong enough in Humanities and they weren't attending office hours to get support from their teacher. But a few weeks after they started working on the truck, their Humanities teacher told me they had started attending office hours, and their writing was improving. After all, if they could convert a truck to electric power through persistence and effort, surely they could pass Humanities.

They graduated that spring.

As this story so clearly illustrates, engaging in the work of making is a highly distributed process. Here, not only did Roberto, Cesar, and Tomas work together as a team, but they also sourced knowledge and expertise from a variety of other individuals. Even beyond their truck conversion project, when the young men realized they needed support passing their Humanities courses, they realized that to achieve their goals, they needed to reach out to their teacher for help. Through a do-it-together process, Roberto, Cesar, and Tomas were able to act on their individual and collective agency (Figure 3.3).

In Chapter Two we discussed the distributed nature of teaching and learning in maker settings. Teachers often tell stories of how students solidify their newly acquired and often fragile knowledge of a skill or technique by teaching what they have just learned to someone else. In this way, students develop an I-can-do-that sense of agency not merely because of an internal decision to be proactive about redesigning, hacking, or tweaking but also because of an engagement with a community

Photo by Aaron Vanderwerff.

FIGURE 3.3: To convert the truck they acquired from gasoline to electric power, Roberto, Cesar, and Tomas had to make many modifications. Here, Cesar helps make room for the electric motor.

and responding to its needs. It is not surprising then that the educators we spoke with both emphasized student agency as a primary outcome of maker-centered learning in Chapter One and suggested that distributed learning was a central practice in the maker-centered classroom in Chapter Two.

To summarize: first, at its core, agency is shaped by choices, intentions, and actions. One can make a distinction between having a sense of agency and agentic action: Having a sense of agency implies having the intention or tendency toward action, but does not necessarily guarantee that the actions one feels empowered to take will necessarily be enacted. Agentic action moves beyond having a *sense* of agency and involves the process of activating—or performing—one's intentions.

Second, in the sphere of maker-centered learning, activating one's agency generally refers to an extensive and complex web of interrelated actions, rather than a single discrete act. And third, maker-centered agentive acts are not simply the output of an individual working solo without context. They are best understood as supported by, and often enacted within, a social context.

Agency and Maker Empowerment

With these ideas as a backdrop, we turn now to the concept of maker empowerment. The purpose of establishing this concept is a practical one: We propose that maker empowerment is a key and desirable outcome of maker-centered learning, and we aim to describe maker empowerment in a way that can usefully inform the day-to-day work that maker educators do when they design, implement, and assess maker-centered learning experiences. Here is how we define it:

> Maker empowerment: *A sensitivity to the designed dimension of objects and systems, along with the inclination and capacity to shape one's world through building, tinkering, re/designing, or hacking.*

It is important to note that the phrase maker empowerment is meant to refer to more than a single instance of action or achievement. As we mentioned earlier, a sense of agency with regard to making—what we are now calling a sense of maker empowerment—is an abiding tendency rather than a rule-defined behavior.

Accordingly, maker empowerment as an educational outcome is a kind of disposition that students develop, a way of being in the world, that is characterized by understanding oneself as a person of resourcefulness who can muster the wherewithal to change things through making. It is not—or at least not merely—a set of technical skills.

In a way, the concept of maker empowerment is similar to the principle of having a bias toward action that is a core tenet of design thinking.[11] Interestingly, the idea of a having bias toward action originally comes from the business world, where it was put forth to characterize a quick decision-making mind-set that could counter the syndrome of paralysis by analysis and cumbersome bureaucratic control.[12] Although paralysis by analysis is certainly something to be avoided, the opposite of maker empowerment—and the syndrome for which the concept is meant to be a corrective—is a bit different.

Being maker *unempowered* is to have a passive consumerist orientation, in which one unreflectively accepts ready-made goods and social systems as they present themselves, without recognizing that it is a choice to do so and that these human-designed objects and systems are susceptible to modification. Moreover, because the concept of maker carries with it the connotation of constructing, assembling, and the fitting together of parts, the idea of maker unempowerment implies a lack of sensitivity to design, and indeed a thoughtless disregard of the designed, form-and-function character of the made world. Perhaps the simplest way to put it is that being maker unempowered suggests that one is blind to the roles others have played in the making of things and therefore blind to the possibility of enacting one's own agency with regard to making.

The concept of maker empowerment is meant to characterize a broad educational outcome of maker-centered learning—an agentic, dispositional outcome that is worthwhile for many types of students. Acquiring a sense of maker empowerment is appropriate not just for students who are already would-be maker types (e.g., hackers, tinkerers, hobbyists) but also for students who, although they may not go on in life to define themselves as makers, will still take the initiative to engage in maker activities from time to time (Figure 3.4). So, for example, a maker-empowered person might be someone who does not think of himself as a maker

FIGURE 3.4: Students at Marymount School of New York take the initiative to do some online research to figure out how to import music from their iTunes into an Arduino-based device they are building.

Photo by Agency *by* Design.

but, after the purchase of a new laptop computer, envisions the perfect laptop cover and endeavors to design and make it rather than purchasing it from a store. It would include the girl who eagerly scours the Internet for instructions on how to make a potato shooter rather than purchasing a ready-made potato rocket online, or the young couple who decide to make their senior prom outfits out of duct tape rather than opting for the traditional formal wear. And of course it wholeheartedly includes people like Jimmy, who tackled the challenge of keeping his backpack alive, and Ana, who tackled the challenge of changing a whole system of book distribution between independent booksellers and underresourced schools.

Empowerment and Social Justice

The foregoing examples mainly bring out the maker side of the phrase maker empowerment. Regarding the term empowerment, we feel it is important to note the long history of empowerment initiatives emanating from the field of youth development. Broadly, the goal of youth empowerment is to help young people develop the ability to make decisions for themselves in a manner that positively affects their own lives and the lives of others. In this sense, the concept of youth empowerment is dispositional in the way that maker empowerment is, but it also has a social justice aspect to it. Although our work would never suggest that maker empowerment is a disposition that develops in isolation, many youth empowerment initiatives specifically respond to social inequities or the imbalance of power within a social system—much in the way that David Clifford referred to earlier in this chapter. And indeed, many youth development programs take on social justice issues by focusing on the empowerment of young people from traditionally disenfranchised communities. In fact, the Abundance Foundation, the primary philanthropic supporter of the Agency *by* Design research initiative, has devoted an entire strand of its resources toward funding just such empowerment initiatives.[13] As the foundation's website states:

> *The Abundance Foundation strives to empower the communities it works with by training leaders, improving safety and providing tools for building stability and greater sustainability. We believe that women and youth are*

disproportionately impacted by war, natural disasters, economic disadvantage and violence. By partnering with organizations who focus on supporting women and youth to create conditions under which they can thrive, the Abundance Foundation helps to create lasting positive change.[14]

As can be seen in this excerpt, empowerment initiatives—whether for youth, women, or others—are situated within greater cultural contexts. Even when such empowerment initiatives are focused on individual youth development, those individuals are always situated within greater social systems.

Youth empowerment initiatives are diverse and can include organizations devoted to civic engagement, youth rights councils, student activism networks, and community organizing initiatives. Many contemporary arts education organizations likewise include a specific focus on youth empowerment combined with a social justice agenda. A general interest in youth empowerment programming has recently manifested itself in the form of what has come to be known as *creative youth development*. A 2014 study frames creative youth development as an instrumental effect of learning in various disciplines:

As young people learn the arts, humanities, and sciences. . . they develop personal, social, and intellectual skills and capacities that are important for their growth and success in life, school, and work. They also use these disciplines as means to understand and change the world around them, to connect to the greater human experience, and to develop and express their own sense of identity.[15]

Though maker empowerment may be seen as a separate brand of agency that is enacted differently in the maker-centered classroom than it is within the context of a youth empowerment or creative youth development program, we believe there are many commonalities between these various settings as well. We also believe that maker-centered learning may itself have much to learn from the work of youth empowerment and creative youth development organizations—especially with regard to considering how imbalanced power structures shape our social experiences, and how one's actions—the things one makes in the world—have the potential to affect the lives of others.

Empowerment in Education

From the standpoint of education, the goal of cultivating a sense of empowerment is nothing new; it is the deep rationale behind much of what we teach. We teach art, or history, or mathematics not solely to the group of students who will go on to make their livings in these areas but to all students because we believe it is empowering for all young people to learn how to engage with the world through the lenses of these disciplines. Although maker-centered learning is not a stand-alone discipline, the concept of maker empowerment aims for this same breadth. Not all students who are exposed to maker education will go on to become scientists, technology specialists, engineers, or carpenters. But perhaps, through high-quality maker-centered learning experiences, they might all acquire a sense of maker empowerment.

If you consider the definition of maker empowerment we previously articulated as a design—and most of the complex concepts humans invent are designs—you can see that it weaves together three distinct ideas. For the sake of convenience, here is the definition again: Maker empowerment is a sensitivity to the designed dimension of objects and systems, along with the inclination and capacity to shape one's world through building, tinkering, re/designing, or hacking. The first phrase, a sensitivity to the designed dimension of objects and systems, points to the importance of simply noticing that many of the objects, ideas, and systems we encounter in the world—from desktops to democracy to driver education classes—are human-made designs. They are composed of specific parts that fit together to serve one or more purposes, and they can be understood and analyzed from the standpoint of design. The second part of the sentence mentions both the inclination and the capacity to make (or remake) things. The terms *inclination* and *capacity* are separated intentionally. Inclination has to do with motivation to do something. Capacity has to do with the skill or wherewithal to actually do it.

This three-part definition, with its emphasis on the triad of sensitivity, inclination, and capacity, extends a concept of dispositional behavior developed at Project Zero that proposes that ability alone is not enough to ensure action.[16] To draw again on our bicycle example, think about what it means to be called a cyclist. It is necessary to have not only the capacity to ride a bicycle but also the motivation to ride a bike on a regular basis and to be alert to occasions to do so. Dispositional behavior, which by definition means the tendency to do something on a regular basis, occurs when these three concepts coalesce—the capacity to do something, the motivation to do it, and the sensitivity to appropriate occasions to do it.

This view of the mechanism of dispositional behavior—often termed the *triadic theory of dispositions*—may sound good in theory. Importantly, it is also supported by empirical research.[17] Through a series of rather elaborate experiments, researchers have shown that the contribution of these three elements—ability, inclination, and sensitivity—can indeed be individually distinguished in young people's intellectual behavior, and that a shortfall in any of the three elements can block cognitive performance. As an example, consider the tendency to think outside the box. People who have this disposition tend to have a distinctive and dependable mind-set that flavors their engagement with the world. They are skilled at challenging existing paradigms and developing break-set ideas (ability); they are interested in innovative ideas and solutions and are motivated to seek them out (inclination); and they are alert to occasions when outside-the-box thinking is called for (sensitivity). If any one or more of these factors are lacking, agentic behavior will not ensue. For instance, ability without motivation will not work—think of how many things we can do but do not do simply because we do not want to do them. Motivation without capacity does not work either—consider all the things we want to do but cannot because we do not have the necessary skills.

What about sensitivity? Here is where it gets interesting. It turns out that the biggest bottleneck to dispositional behavior—in other words, the shortfall that most frequently prevents ability, inclination, and sensitivity from coalescing into regular patterns of action—is a shortfall of sensitivity. In other words, at least in terms of critical and creative thinking, young people do not follow through with these habits of mind not because they cannot (ability) and not because they do not want to (inclination) but mainly because they do not notice opportunities to do so (sensitivity). This finding does not mean that young people's inner detection mechanisms are hopelessly flawed. Sensitivity has everything to do with the saliency of cues in the environment. If an environment does not have strong cues toward certain patterns of behavior—or actually contains countercues—it can be pretty hard for those patterns of behavior to be internalized by young people acting within that environment.

The Project Zero research on dispositional behavior just described was originally conducted to investigate thinking dispositions—habits of mind like open-mindedness, reason-seeking, and perspective taking—and it took place in fairly traditional school settings, so perhaps the findings about a lack of sensitivity are not surprising: Schools typically cue students to think in certain ways at certain times rather than encourage them to be alert to occasions to determine what to think about on their own. For example, at 10:00 a.m. students might be asked to start thinking about math and then at 10:45 a.m. to redirect their attention to thinking about art. We cannot know for sure if the findings about sensitivity transfer to the notion of developing a disposition toward maker empowerment, but it is easy to see that there are lots of cues in our everyday environments that prompt us not to notice design and not to make things on our own: The endless stream of cheap, ready-made objects; a culture of disposable goods; entrenched social systems that seem impervious to change; and little time for—or valuing of—prolonged tinkering or iterative cycles of experimentation with materials.

Maker culture is different, of course. What goes on inside makerspaces and in maker-centered classrooms is usually just the opposite, and that is part of the point. Maker-centered learning experiences often explicitly aim to cultivate students' sensitivity to the made dimensions of the world, for instance by encouraging them to become alert to design, and by urging them to notice not only that much of our world is designed by humans, but that our human-made designs—the objects and systems all around us—are susceptible to change (Figure 3.5).

Earlier in this chapter we introduced Jimmy, the young man who hacked his backpack, and Ana, the young woman who developed a new distribution system for providing a school in San Francisco with a fresh supply of books. The accomplishments of both of these young people can be seen through the lens of maker empowerment. Both of them had the inclination to change or fix something in their worlds: Jimmy was motivated by the desire to continue to use his way cool backpack, just as Ana was motivated by her desire to put books in the hands of children

FIGURE 3.5: Students look closely at environmental systems to design devices for taking trash out of the water as part of a larger unit on the effect of pollution in local waterways.

who would not have had access to them otherwise. Both Jimmy and Ana ended up having the skills they needed to get their respective jobs done, although it was noteworthy that they both developed the requisite skills along the way: Jimmy learned how to sew a zipper; Ana learned how to fundraise and connect disparate members of her community.

Very importantly, both of these young people were sensitive to an opportunity to engage with the designed dimensions of their worlds. Jimmy personalized his backpack, modifying its design even before it was in need of repair. Ana saw the absence of books in certain settings not just as a regrettable situation and an unjust social imbalance but also as a flaw in the design of a larger system that she decided to address herself. As mentioned earlier, a lack of sensitivity to opportunity is a significant obstacle to the development of dispositional behavior, and one that is often overlooked. With this in mind, if maker empowerment is a desirable dispositional outcome for maker-centered learning, then it is crucial to pay special attention to helping young people develop a sensitivity to opportunity. We turn to this theme in the next chapter, where we ask: How can we help young people become sensitive to opportunities that activate their sense of maker empowerment? That is, how can we help young people become more sensitive to the designed dimensions of their worlds?

Developing a Sensitivity to Design

In Melissa Butler's kindergarten class at Pittsburgh Allegheny K–5 school in Pittsburgh, Pennsylvania, students spend a whole class period focused on one screw. With their small hands, each child holds it, examines it, sketches it, turns it around, and sketches it some more. The children rotate the screw to get different perspectives and see new angles. Each student feels the screw's intricacies, discusses its complexities, and notices that their neighbors' screws look slightly different than their own. For 25 minutes the students are focused and curious. At no point do they say that they are done with their screw or wonder what to look at next; as Melissa noted in a conversation following the class, they understand that "there's always more to see."

Why spend an entire class period looking at a screw? Because in that 25 minutes of quiet exploration, two important shifts happen. First, students begin to understand that objects as seemingly simple as screws are actually remarkably complex. Second, they learn that the way one child sees a screw is not necessarily the way another child may see it. In Chapter Three we suggested that students' everyday environments often do not cue them to notice design. Exercises like this one—exercises that allow and value the time and space needed to sit with and reflect on an object—can help alert young people to the designed dimensions of their worlds.

Students in Melissa's class have been participating in the Children's Innovation Project. Cofounded by Melissa Butler and Jeremy Boyle in 2010, the Children's Innovation Project brings technology and circuitry into early childhood and elementary education. Children learn how electricity works and come to understand its language and symbolic systems. Yet the goal of these classroom visits is not merely for students to acquire inert knowledge about electricity. Instead, technology is introduced as a material through which young people can explore and interact with the world and recognize where and how they might be able to shape it. The exercise of looking at a screw is a starting point, laying important groundwork for young learners to recognize a world of design—a world of parts, wholes, sequences, and interactions. Whether looking at an object like a screw or exploring an entire electronic system, the experiences that the Children's Innovation Project offers are about encouraging curiosity and stimulating a desire to understand and engage with the world (Figure 4.1).

Look carefully at the screw. Draw what you see. Try again from a new perspective.

Photo by Children's Innovation Project

FIGURE 4.1: Students engage in some close looking at a screw as part of the Children's Innovation Project learning in Pittsburgh Public Schools.

For Melissa and Jeremy, opportunities to look closely and explore the complexity of objects and systems are necessary to build a cohort of young people who are critical thinkers. Their work with the Children's Innovation Project provides a visible link between noticing design and fostering a sense of maker empowerment in their students. To attain this sense of maker empowerment it is critical for Melissa and Jeremy's students to be deeply curious about their environments. To understand a single screw is to spend ample time looking at it, exploring its parts, thinking about how other people might experience the screw, and situating the screw in the many systems it is a part of. As Jeremy noted, to understand a single screw is for a student to realize that "something like a screw is not just one thing, and the way that I may see it isn't necessarily the way it is." As Jeremy described, understanding the multidimensionality of simple objects—and viewing them from multiple perspectives—helps students to "appreciate how other people see things." Jeremy underscores the value for students in becoming aware "that everything is constructed, that every single thing around you is made and can be viewed from different perspectives. We would like the children we work with to know that all of the things around them have been constructed." In this chapter we name the understanding of the constructed nature of the world that the Children's Innovation Project aims to support as having a *sensitivity to design*.

Developing a Sensitivity to Design in a Consumer-Driven World

The previous chapter posed the question: How might we help young people become sensitive to opportunities to activate their sense of maker empowerment? In other words, how can young people be encouraged to notice opportunities to build, tinker, hack, or re/design the objects and systems in their worlds? One answer is to encourage young people to see that their worlds are largely composed of objects and systems that have been designed, and that these designs can be tinkered with or entirely reimagined. This may seem easy to do. After all, young people engage with human-conceived and human-made objects and systems every day, so it seems natural that they would reflect on their form and function to some degree. But young people live within the same cultural climate that adults do—a climate that often seems to support consumer passivity and a disengagement from design. Many of the objects people use each day prevent them from understanding how they work; technological devices and programs think for us; the economy and efficiency of manufacturing inspires a throwaway, consumable relationship to stuff. Moreover, the fast-paced and fully scheduled nature of day-to-day life in the early 2000s leaves many of us with little time to look at the screw in the way that Jeremy and Melissa's students do. The result? A growing culture of consumerism that is becoming increasingly more distanced from the made dimensions of our worlds. Two factors that contribute to this distancing include the functional inaccessibility of contemporary gadgets and gizmos and a growing acceptance of life within a throwaway culture.

The Hidden Mechanics of Stuff

Many of the objects that people use today lack transparency. The slick shells of many of our favorite devices do not invite one to see how the parts hidden beneath them work. Consider the difference between typing on a contemporary laptop computer and using a traditional typewriter. On a typewriter, one can observe the process of hitting a key and watching a lever engage another lever to push a type hammer through a ribbon and strike a paper rolled around a platen, leaving a black

Photos by Agency by Design.

FIGURE 4.2: Students at the Harvard Graduate School of Education consider the designed properties and inner workings of an old Smith-Corona typewriter.

letter in its wake (Figure 4.2). The carriage moves one space to the left, ensuring a fresh place on the paper on which to type. A screwdriver might be needed to remove the top shell of a typewriter in order to watch this happen, but the opportunity is made evident thanks to the use of standard screws. A laptop computer is another story. Not only is it difficult to discern how striking a keyboard results in letters appearing on a screen, but there is also no invitation to take a laptop apart. In other words, there is no obvious opportunity for one to get inside a computer to better understand how it works.

Of course, sometimes a smooth outer shell is part of the aesthetic design of an object—a choice intended to make it more visually appealing or pleasing to touch. And at other times an outer shell is in place for safety purposes—to protect curious fingers from the quick-moving mechanical parts inside. But when the means to peer underneath the shell of an object are intentionally obscured, an object can seem to be designed to keep the curious at bay. The technology company Apple has come under fire for this for years. With their smooth, seemingly impenetrable outer surfaces, Apple laptops, tablets, and smartphones have been called out for their intentionally designed lack of hackability. In fact, in 2014 Kyle Wiens, the cofounder and CEO of iFixit, an online repair community, noted that the newly released MacBook Pro with retina display was the "least repairable laptop we've ever taken apart." He explained:

> Unlike the previous model, the display is fused to the glass, which means replacing the LCD requires buying an expensive display assembly. The RAM is now soldered to the logic board—making future memory upgrades impossible. And the battery is glued to the case, requiring customers to mail their laptop to Apple every so often for a $200 replacement. The design may well be comprised of "highly recyclable aluminum and glass"—but my friends in the electronics recycling industry tell me they have no way of recycling aluminum that has glass glued to it like Apple did with both this machine and the recent iPad.[1]

Not only is it difficult to engage with the internal workings of Apple products, but once inside it is also not an encouraging place for a novice to tinker, hack, or otherwise poke around to see how things work. To be fair, Apple often responds to the demands of the market. And in many cases, as Wiens later explained, the market's demand for the light, portable MacBook Air series (on which much of this book has been written) superseded consumers' interests in having access to the insides of their devices. As a result, the hidden inner workings of one's technological devices may squelch one's inclination to understand how gadgets and gizmos work.

But these obstacles to understanding the inner mechanics of things are not restricted to technology; they prevail with less tech-oriented objects as well. An example of the distant relationship many of us have with the inner workings of the stuff in our lives can be found in a 2013 TEDx talk conducted by Jennifer Oxman Ryan, a researcher on the Agency *by* Design team.[2] During Jennifer's talk she asked how many people in the audience had used a doorknob that day. Not surprisingly, nearly everyone had. Also not surprisingly, most had never asked themselves how a doorknob really works: How do the parts mesh together? What internal mechanisms allow the knob to turn and the latch assembly and tumbler to function properly? A doorknob is something many of us use several times a day, yet very few people take the time to look closely at the doorknobs in their worlds to better understand how they work.

Living in the Throes of a Throwaway Culture

Culturally, many of us have come to accept that electronics are consumable products with limited life spans rather than objects that invite tinkering or hacking. Swept up in a system of constantly changing accessories and ports (and new software releases that require more computing power), consumers are encouraged to replace their devices altogether rather than fix them or buy replacement parts when they crash or require increased capacity.

On a less technological level, even the mechanical products in our lives have become increasingly less hackable—and therefore less fixable. Rivets have replaced screws in household objects such as eggbeaters and stepladders, necessitating their replacement—in lieu of their repair—when they break. It is no surprise then, that two of the popular mantras associated with the maker movement are "Screws, not glues!" and "If you can't open it you don't own it, it owns you."

In *Things Come Apart*, Todd McLellan's photography book celebrating the careful dissection of everyday objects, contributor Kyle Wiens called into question life within a throwaway culture. He argued that, rather than repair objects when they fail, the developed world tends to discard them. For Wiens, this move ends up "squandering the years of work and thought and mining and manufacturing that went into them."[3] Not trying to fix a thing by taking it apart precludes the people who use it from discovering how it was put together in the first place. Wiens continued by asking, "What happens when we do not know how things work? We are cut off, trapped in a modern wasteland where we can only try to solve problems with our credit cards rather than with our hands and brains."[4]

Imagine the learning that would take place if one tried to fix a broken doorknob? One would have to take each piece apart, thereby revealing the interactions between the knob, tumbler, and latch. Although it may be easier to simply call a locksmith to do the work,[5] there is much to learn by engaging in this process.

Of course, the flip side of this argument is that it is more efficient to go about one's daily business interacting with objects and systems that one may not fully understand. Sure, many of us may have a superficial understanding of how turning a knob on the stove can heat a burner, but how many of us really need to understand the ignition system at work inside? Does one really need to know how a vacuum cleaner works, or the physics involved in using a spray bottle? If one can successfully get through the day without having to understand how everything works, what is the problem? For Wiens, "Understanding the things we own allows us to do what we do best: solve problems."[6] Wiens's comment underscores the theory of maker empowerment: To understand how the designed components of the world work, and who and what they impact, is to be able to activate a sense of agency, to assert control over the environment so that one may assume an active rather than a passive role in life.

Having this sense of agency, of course, requires noticing design in the first place. Like adults, young people have no lack of opportunity to engage with design: From the sneakers they wear each day to lunch boxes they carry to school, and from the books they use in the classroom to the cell phones they use to text and chat, students are surrounded by human-designed stuff. But unless young people are provided with opportunities to notice and think about these designs, they may not become alert to the complexity of the made dimensions of their worlds (Figure 4.3).

Photo by Jeanine Harmon

FIGURE 4.3: Engaged in a making activity, a student from Emerson Elementary School pauses to examine the properties of the materials he's working with.

What Is a Sensitivity to Design?

So what does it mean to develop a sensitivity to design? Perhaps the first place to start is to define the word *design*. On the surface, the term is straightforward: This book has used the word numerous times so far, and chances are you have always known what is meant. A laptop, a chair, a doorknob, a cell phone—these are all recognizably designed objects. But what makes them so?

Our Project Zero colleague David Perkins has thought deeply about this question, and in his book, *Knowledge as Design*, he explained design this way:

> *A design is a structure adapted to a purpose. Sometimes a single person conceives that structure and its purpose—Benjamin Franklin as the inventor*

of the lightning rod. Sometimes a structure gets shaped to a purpose gradually over time, through the ingenuity of many individuals—the ballpoint pen as a remote descendent of the quill pen. Sometimes a structure gets adapted by a relatively blind process of social evolution, as with customs and languages that reflect human psychological and cultural needs.[7]

This explanation of design is elegant in both its expansiveness and precision. It accommodates designs intended for one purpose and created by one person, as well as designs whose structures are brought into being by many people and whose purposes are emergent rather than intentional. Although Perkins did not spell it out in the previous excerpt, elsewhere in the book he makes it clear that designs often have many purposes, just as they often have many parts and many authors. The core characteristic that unites the huge range of objects and systems that qualify as design is that they all have at least some non-random element that has been shaped to serve a purpose. As Perkins points out, a design is not "a regular pattern that serves no particular purpose, as in ripples on sand dunes."[8] His example refers to the aesthetically pleasing features that occur in the world by chance, but the point extends to any features that occur without purpose. Like the ripples on a sand dune, a random heap of trash is not a design, though many of the items within the heap may well be.

With David Perkins's definition of design as a backdrop, we return again to the question of what it means to have a sensitivity to design. We offer the following definition:

Sensitivity to design: *Being attuned to the designed dimension of objects and systems, with an understanding that the designed world is malleable.*

There are two parts to this definition, and each deserves explanation. The first part, being attuned to the designed dimension of objects and systems, builds on Perkins's definition of design to suggest that a sensitivity to design means noticing the made aspect of things—how the parts and pieces of things fit together and are adapted to serve certain purposes. The second part of the definition, understanding that the designed world is malleable, emphasizes the importance of being aware that it is possible for designs to be reimagined or repurposed to be different than they are. This last point is especially important in the context of maker-centered learning because it connects to the sense of agency that maker educators are so keen to develop in their students: Understanding that a design is malleable means that it is possible to envision changing it.

Throughout contemporary Western culture, designs are in plain sight everywhere one looks—from the dwellings we live in to the form of government we live under to the clothes we wear. So even if one were to acknowledge that a sensitivity to design is a good thing to have, it is reasonable to ask why it is necessary to cultivate it: Doesn't a sensitivity to design just come about as a matter of course? Part of the answer to this question has already been suggested earlier in this chapter. Precisely because designs are so ubiquitous, they often seem invisible. In the fast pace of everyday life many of us rarely stop to notice the designs we use, let alone consider how they work or how they are made. Moreover, the slick outer surfaces of some contemporary designs are often intended to keep the curious from probing their inner workings. And our consumer culture, with its throwaway approach to goods, discourages us from fixing things when they are broken and thus learning about design through tinkering and repair.

Still, it is possible to argue that maker-centered learning addresses this problem because students' attention is directed to design through the very act of making. Building a chair, mending a knapsack, creating a book distribution system—these are all activities that require attention to design. But while it is true that maker activities require students to pay attention to design in the moment, it is less clear that they encourage students to transfer this sensitivity to new contexts.

In this respect, maker-centered classroom activities are not all that different from other school-based activities. Recall the notion of maker empowerment put forth in the previous chapter. It proposed that maker empowerment is an important goal of maker-centered learning and that it is a dispositional goal, in that it emphasizes a way of seeing and being in the world rather than a discrete set of skills. The chapter discussed the concept of maker empowerment in the context of a larger theory of dispositional behavior that described dispositions as being activated by the coalescence of three factors: the ability to act in a certain way, the inclination to do so, and the sensitivity to occasions when such actions are called for.

The chapter further pointed out that the reason sensitivity is a special challenge in educational contexts is because classroom activities tend to function as a substitute for sensitivity. For example, consider an in-school maker-centered learning class in which students are learning to make soft circuitry clothing—scarves and hats and shirts that glimmer with LED lights and emit sounds as they move. With a bit of instruction and the right materials, students will easily be able to make these things (ability). And they will probably enjoy the work and be motivated to engage in it (inclination). But the very fact that the class exists and that the activity has been explicitly offered up to students as a learning opportunity removes the need for students to find the opportunity on their own.

This is perfectly natural in a school setting. To an extent, it is one of the main purposes of school—to engage students in learning activities that they might not naturally engage in otherwise. But it means that attention to sensitivity does not necessarily get addressed in school. The counterargument, of course, is that it does not need to be addressed, because as long as school does a good job of teaching (and testing) students' ability to do certain things—calculate the volume of a cube, interpret a poem, build a chair—students will naturally see opportunities to transfer these abilities on their own, right?

Well, maybe. But not reliably, which is what the research on dispositions has shown: Students often have both the ability to use certain skills and the inclination to do so, but simply do not notice occasions to do so. These findings are consistent with a larger body of educational research on the transfer of knowledge that shows that people transfer knowledge from one context to another far less frequently than might be expected.[9] This is one of the reasons that students may perform well on tests but do not necessarily think to use their test-cued knowledge in the flow of everyday life.

To sum up, the argument for why we as educators should pay attention to cultivating students' sensitivity to design is, first, that maker empowerment, which is a broad goal of maker-centered learning, is a dispositional outcome. Second, like any disposition, it is activated when three elements coalesce—ability, inclination, and sensitivity. Third, sensitivity to design is the specific brand of sensitivity that is relevant to maker empowerment. In other words, to feel empowered to change the world through making, one has to first notice that the objects and systems of daily life are designs—that is, that they are structures adapted to purposes—and that because they are designs, they could possibly be made differently. Fourth, formal instructional settings tend to stand in for sensitivity, so students do not necessarily learn how to notice occasions to activate their abilities outside of specialized contexts. To be sure, maker activities are often vivid, fun, and intrinsically engaging. And because they may be more memorable than drier school subjects, they may do a better job of cuing students to transfer their maker abilities to new contexts. But everything we know about dispositional behavior suggests that we ought not to count on students developing a sensitivity to design as a matter of course without taking a closer look.

How Are Students Sensitive (or Not) to Design?

An interesting fact about cultivating a sensitivity to anything—design included—is that a lot can be accomplished by simply asking people to be alert to things they may otherwise not notice. For example, suppose someone challenged you to notice all the insects that crossed your path on your daily walk to work. Just by shifting your attention a little bit you would almost certainly notice lots of ants and flies and spiders you had not seen before. In this spirit, the Agency *by* Design research team wanted to know what students would simply notice on their own if they were explicitly asked to notice the designs around them.

To explore this question, in 2012 our research team collaborated with a group of educators in Oakland, California. The goal of this particular strand of inquiry was to better understand what students noticed, and also what they did not notice, about the designed dimensions of their worlds. To find out, our teacher partners asked their students to go on a design hunt in and around their schools. They framed the task like this: Write down anything you notice that has been designed by people. You may write a list or describe what you see or draw a picture.

Of course this was a very open-ended task: As one student noted, "That's going to be everything, like a million things, everywhere." And in fact, students noticed many, many designed objects: trash cans, staplers, coffee mugs, backpacks, glasses, lunchboxes, gardens, sneakers. This may seem like a simple, if not obvious, finding. But it was interesting to note what students' lists did not include. During the design hunt, almost no one wrote about or drew the lunch line, the sidewalk they used to get to school, the arrival or dismissal process, or the fire drill system. Students easily noticed designed objects, but they did not seem to notice designed systems.

Of course, students did not entirely overlook the designed systems in their environments. One student, for example, identified a computer game as a designed string of data. Nonetheless, despite the rare examples of students noticing designed systems, what we came to understand was that when asked to notice design most students focused their attention on objects.

This curious finding made us wonder what would happen if students were explicitly prompted to notice the systems in their worlds. So, in a second exercise, our teacher partners asked their students to go on another design hunt but this time to choose one designed item they noticed earlier and think about the kinds of systems that it might be a part of. As it turned out, students were very good at thinking about designed systems when prompted to do so. Indeed, some of their observations were quite nuanced. As an example, here is the story of Nala, a twelfth-grade student at Oakland International High School.[10]

In her initial design hunt, Nala identified her personal computer as a designed object. In the second activity, she identified her computer as being an object situated within broader systems. Nala described various primary systems such as the Internet, subsystems such as social media platforms, and broader super systems such as networked communication between people, and she did this while recognizing that a computer is a system composed of the various subsystems (e.g., hardware components and software applications) that make it work. Notably, her ideas about systems went beyond unidirectional causality (i.e., A causes B which then causes C, and so on. . .), which might be expected to be the most common way to think about systems. Rather, simply by being prompted to think about systems, Nala seemed to surface the many layers, complex interactions, and intricacies associated with designed systems.

Though Nala was a senior in high school at the time of this exercise, we also found that even quite young children were able to see and describe the designed dimension of systems. For example, one kindergarten student at Emerson Elementary School described the designed properties of an apple pie and provided a drawn narrative of the systems involved in transforming apples into dessert. Yet another student honed in on the role of a trashcan (a designed object) and told a linear narrative about the trashcan's journey to the dump (a designed system).

This informal experiment, in which students conducted first a design hunt and then followed it up with a systems hunt, suggested to us that students of all ages are able to think about the design of objects and of systems with nuance and depth. We are by no means the first educators to notice this. For instance, veteran systems educator Linda Booth Sweeney has written extensively about this topic, noting that even preschool-aged children can understand the general concept of systems.[11] Our work intends to expand on earlier articulations of young people's ability to understand complex systems by first drawing attention to the idea that activating students' capacity to notice the designed dimensions of objects and systems may simply require some explicit provocation, and second by suggesting that learning to notice systems as designs is an important part of developing a sensitivity to design. That systems can be hard to pick out from the flow of everyday life as designs is easy to understand. After all, the objects many of us engage with each day are themselves systems that are composed of subsystems that are also situated within greater supersystems. Nala's experience illustrates this point. A computer is a system composed of subsystems, which is also situated within the greater supersystems that Nala identified. It is hard to put boundaries around a system, but it is well worth trying to do so because of the understanding it yields, as Nala's story illustrates. Helping learners discern systems and explore them as designs has been a rich throughline in the work of Agency *by* Design, and in the next chapter we offer several examples of what this looks like in practice. But first, a few more words about cultivating a sensitivity to design.

Seeing the Designed World as Malleable

Recall the first part of the definition of sensitivity to design offered earlier, which emphasized the importance of being attuned to the designed dimension of objects and systems. The design hunt and systems hunt described above both speak to this part of the definition by showing what students can notice simply by being asked. This is important because it gives us a baseline by which to think of educational interventions. The second part of the definition emphasized understanding that the designed world is malleable. To bring this aspect of sensitivity to design into relief we take a different tack and offer two examples from the adult world. The first comes from one of Agency *by* Design's Oakland-based teacher partners; the second comes from the work of the Cuban artist Ernesto Oroza.

When Tatum Omari first joined up with Agency *by* Design, she was a teacher at the North Oakland Community Charter School. Along with other teacher collaborators in the area, Tatum participated in workshops and did activities with her students that involved noticing, and hacking, the designs of objects and systems. After several months of avid and inspired involvement with the program, Tatum shared the following story—a story of parenting, design awareness, system hacking, and the true value of seeing the world through the lens of maker empowerment.

Having arrived at her daughter's first day of soccer practice, Tatum noticed that, though she had remembered shin guards and socks, her daughter was wearing sparkly party shoes instead of sneakers. She described the utter feeling of disappointment, aware of the inevitability of having let her daughter down. Rather than abandoning the practice, or running to the nearest store for new kicks, Tatum did a quick on-the-field assessment of her situation: "Maybe the sparkly party shoes are different from most?" she asked herself. "Maybe she could run in them?" A quick test sprint by her daughter told a different story, as "both shoes flew off before she took her third step." But rather than panic, that is when the systems redesigning began. As Tatum explained:

> . . .But then I had a thought—I eyed the shin guards and socks my daughter was carrying and had a revelation. "I've got it!" I thought to myself. It was time for a system redesign. . . .
>
> I took a careful look at the system of soccer gear my daughter had with her. Normally the shin guards go on first and then the socks go over them. Next would come the stable tennis shoes or cleats—not *sparkly flats*. We didn't have the tennis shoes or cleats, so some way, somehow we had to make the sparkly flats work. "To hack this system we are going to need to put things on

in a different order," I said. I realized that the shin guards had that awesome little strap that goes underneath the foot. "If we put your socks on, then the sparkly flats, and then put the shin guards over everything—maybe the shin guards will hold your shoes on," I said to my daughter. . . .

I used what I had learned about systems to take a serious look at the parts and purposes of my daughter's soccer gear. Yes, I was missing a pretty integral part of the soccer get-up but by analyzing what I had to work with and doing a little redesign, the kid still got to play soccer.[12]

In this vignette, Tatum was able to quickly solve a problem by slowing down and critically analyzing her situation. At first pass, having her daughter participate in soccer practice wearing sparkly flats that would not stay on seemed a fairly risky endeavor. However, Tatum took the time to explore the design of her daughter's practice clothes. She noticed the details and nuances of each element and also how the components worked together. She paused for looking, reflecting, and gaining an understanding of how she might problem-solve without purchasing new gear or abandoning the situation. Securing the sparkly flats with the strap of the shin guards allowed for a reconceptualized system that would not result in a flyaway shoe.

Tatum tells a playful story, but the message is absolutely on point: Maker empowerment is about seeing the designed world as malleable and not being subject to the constraints of a particular situation. By being attuned to design it is possible to see opportunity to effect change, or in Tatum's case, to solve a problem with a simple hack.

Far removed from Tatum's dilemma with sparkly shoes on the soccer field, Cuban artist Ernesto Oroza's concept of *technological disobedience* provides a quite different example of what it means to see the designed world as malleable.[13] Oroza's technological disobedience project offers a curated collection of repurposed objects created in Cuba during a time of economic turmoil. As he has described, beginning in the 1960s the Cuban government became increasingly more isolated from the industrialized world and, as a result of U.S. embargoes, began to experience an immense decline in new technology and equipment entering the island nation. As a result, Cubans needed to find a way to work against a system that was not working for them—and learn to make the vehicles, appliances, and electronics of everyday life by themselves. "From the endless, ongoing restoration of the iconic 1950s Buicks to the creation of baby toys made from milk cans and dried beans," Oroza explained, "fabricating goods not officially available on the island became an essential skill."[14]

Typical artifacts borne of this time included TV antennas created from aluminum food trays, electric lighters built of pens and light bulbs, shoe polishers and key cutters fashioned from old dryer motors, and battery rechargers constructed from the electronic components stripped from old radios. As Oroza explained:

> The tops of penicillin vials have become the best solution for valves on pressure cookers. Deodorant canisters proved excellent electrical switches (close the lid to turn the electricity on!). Defective fluorescent tubes now make up 3-D picture frames. An old 33-rpm vinyl, cut properly, would serve as a fan blade—and its creators could reproduce copies of it. An old and deteriorated Eagle kerosene lamp reappeared when power outages became common, and sometimes a milk bottle or gas tank functioned as the lampshade. Each creation's new appearance and new function made it unique.[15]

Cubans became master hackers as they became further independent from the singular purposes and limited life spans of the Western-made devices decaying all around them. In addition to the ingenuity expressed by many Cubans during this time, Oroza also explained that, through the process of becoming master hackers, many Cubans developed a sensitivity to design and a new way of seeing the objects and systems in the world that fueled their maker empowerment:

> While reinventing their lives, an unconscious mentality emerged. As a surgeon becomes desensitized to wounds, Cubans became desensitized to designed objects. They stopped seeing the original purpose of the object; instead it became a sample of parts. This is the first Cuban expression of disobedience in their relationship with objects—a growing disrespect for an object's identity and for the truth and authority it embodies.

> After opening, breaking, repairing, and using them so often at their convenience, the makers ultimately disregarded the signs that make occidental objects a unity, a closed identity. Cubans do not fear the emanating authority that brands like Sony, Swatch, or even NASA, command. If something is broken, it will be fixed—somehow. If it could even be conceived as usable to repair other objects, they might as well save it, either in parts or in its entirety. A new future awaits.[16]

As ingenious as the Cubans' hacked-together inventions were, it is important to note that the sensitivity to design expressed by Cubans was not only limited to objects. In the wake of the country's revolution and the onset of Fidel Castro's communist regime, Cubans also became sensitive to the design of the government structure which thrust so many of them into poverty. "The technological disobedience—which the revolution promoted as an alternative to the country's stalled productive sector," Oroza explained, "became the most reliable resource for Cubans to navigate the inefficiencies of the state political system."[17] In this way, Cubans were hacking not only their old Buicks, lunch trays, and aerosol canisters but also a system of oppression.

It is startling to think how the Cuban practice of technological disobedience contrasts with the concept of planned obsolescence that is so pervasive throughout contemporary Western culture. From early marketing strategies designed to convince consumers of the need to frequently replace objects big and small to product models that are explicitly designed to have a limited life span, the industrialized world's history of consumerism has long devalued the notion of objects having longevity and sustainability. A cultural climate of readily made one-off objects, of disposable goods, of consumerism, of a non–fix-it mentality, work to suppress the inclination to notice, let alone tinker with, the many designed objects and systems so many of us engage with everyday. But as Tatum's soccer kit scenario and the Cuban practice of technological disobedience illustrate, by developing a sensitivity to design and seeing the world as malleable, it is possible to acquire a more maker-empowered worldview.

As we have discussed, the many maker educators and thought leaders we have had the privilege to speak with over the past several years have endeavored to do just that: to help their students see themselves as the makers of their experiences, not just consumers of the objects and systems they interact with on a daily basis; to feel they have the capacity and the right to tinker with the designed dimensions of their worlds.

In this chapter we have made the case that an important part of developing students' overall sense of maker empowerment is cultivating their sensitivity to design. In the next chapter, we offer a practical instructional framework for doing so, a suite of cognitive tools to support the framework's core components, and examples of the framework in action.

5

Maker-Centered Teaching and Learning in Action

The preceding chapters introduced the twin concepts of *maker empowerment* and *sensitivity to design* and argued that one of the great promises of maker-centered learning is its potential to empower students to notice, redesign, and reinvent the designed dimensions of their worlds. This chapter presents a framework for cultivating a sensitivity to design and kindling maker empowerment. This framework is comprised of what we have come to believe are three primary maker capacities: looking closely, exploring complexity, and finding opportunity. Here we describe each of these inter-related capacities in detail. We also present several pictures of practice—illustrations of classroom practice and student work—that demonstrate what these maker capacities look like in action. The chapter concludes by considering the kinds of instructional tools and techniques that can support and sustain maker-centered thinking, learning, and teaching. In particular, we propose a suite of four thinking routines designed specifically for the maker-centered classroom.

Before diving into the chapter, we want to acknowledge the dedication and commitment of our teacher colleagues whose work we share herein. The many pictures of practice that follow are drawn from the educators with whom we have closely worked over the course of the Agency *by* Design research project. They include prekindergarten through twelfth-grade teachers from a selection of public, private, and charter schools in Oakland, California: Claremont Middle School, Emerson Elementary School, North Oakland Community Charter School, Oakland International High School, Oakland Technical High School, and Park Day School.

While the group's membership shifted over the years, a core team of educators remained constant. Collectively, this group of dedicated educators came to be known as the Oakland Learning Community.

These educators came from a variety of teaching contexts, including but not limited to drama and technology, kindergarten, fifth-grade social studies, sixth-grade science, and high school arts. Only one of the teachers in the original Oakland Learning Community identified as a maker educator. For her, as well as the others, the challenge was to come to a personal understanding of maker-centered learning and how it could be woven into the curriculum. After several years of close collaboration with these Oakland-based educators, we broadened our work with practitioners and began working with a cadre of national maker educators. These educators were generous with their time, ideas, and feedback.

Although only a small portion of our teacher partners' work is highlighted below, the entire group contributed to our understanding of the emergent maker landscape and helped to develop instructional tools and techniques. Working collaboratively with these practitioners, we pilot-tested ideas, developed tools and resources, and learned from the work that they engaged in with their students. As a result, we began to understand some of the tensions associated with maker-centered learning and explored how these tensions could be addressed at the classroom level.

Though the following pictures of practice are presented as succinct snapshots of teaching and learning experiences, each classroom illustration should be understood as part of a trajectory of work conducted over time and explicitly designed to explore the various elements of maker empowerment.

A Framework for Maker Empowerment

In the previous chapter we made the case that cultivating young people's sensitivity to design plays a primary role in helping them develop a sense of maker empowerment. It should be no surprise then, that cultivating a sensitivity to design is the central focus of our pedagogical framework for maker-centered learning.

Chapter Four defined a sensitivity to design as being attuned to the designed dimension of objects and systems, with an understanding that the designed world is malleable. The framework presented in this chapter identifies three teachable capacities that support the development of a sensitivity to design: looking closely, exploring complexity, and finding opportunity. As Figure 5.1 illustrates, these three interrelated maker capacities form the foundation for our pedagogical framework for maker-centered learning.

We believe that the capacities to look closely, explore complexity, and find opportunity not only provide a critical foundation for developing a sensitivity to design but are also important in all phases of making, designing, or redesigning. It is our hope that by nurturing these maker capacities in young people they may acquire a design-sensitive orientation toward the world—a way of seeing, understanding, and engaging with the built environment. As Figure 5.1 suggests, these three maker capacities interact with one another in a mutually reinforcing, non-linear way. But to understand them as an interrelated whole, we find it helpful to first discuss each capacity individually.

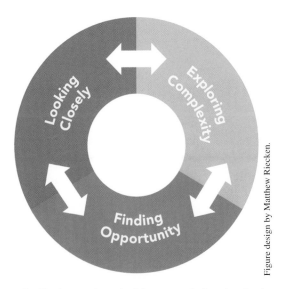

Figure design by Matthew Riecken.

FIGURE 5.1: The Agency *by* Design pedagogical framework for developing a sensitivity to design foregrounds three interrelated maker capacities: looking closely, exploring complexity, and finding opportunity.

Looking Closely

Looking closely is about close, careful, and mindful observation . It often requires sustained time in front of an object or system, to look again and again to notice each intricacy, each nuance, each detail. To look closely is to see what is in front of oneself, to look with focus, to make statements about what something looks like, what it is made of, how it is put together. As Agency *by* Design researcher Shari Tishman has written elsewhere, looking closely "means taking the time to carefully observe more than meets the eye at first glance. It implies lingering, looking long, being generous, almost lavish, with one's attentional focus, in order to see beyond first impressions."[1]

Looking Closely at Computers with English Language Learners at Oakland International High School

In the previous chapter we offered a snapshot of Melissa Butler's classroom in Pittsburgh, Pennsylvania, in which her kindergarten students looked long and closely at a screw. Meanwhile, across the country Thi Bui, a technology teacher at Oakland International High School, launched into a unit with her class of English

FIGURE 5.2: Students in Thi Bui's technology class at Oakland International High School look closely at a computer by taking it apart.

Language Learners aimed at building their comfort with computers (Figure 5.2). Thi's objective was to empower students to confidently problem-solve their own computer issues. To do so, Thi designed a lesson that encouraged students to look closely at computers, inside and out. As she explained:

> I wanted to instill a confidence in students, so that they could remain calm in the face of computer-related issues and problem-solve around them. I found that opening up a computer changed the blind fear that many of them had into something more like curiosity about what all the parts were for. That curiosity led to questions, and questions led to research, more questions, and finally some understanding, familiarity, and confidence. I also wanted to encourage student-driven inquiry, whether it was self-reflection or curiosity about how computers work.

> It is a huge help to empower students to troubleshoot computer problems, if only very basic ones like checking to see whether cables are connected instead of immediately crying, "Miss! My computer doesn't work!"

Thi's first step toward encouraging her students to feel more comfortable and confident was to build awareness of the physical workings of computers. She asked students to begin naming or drawing the parts they discovered, and then to note questions as they arose. She asked students to connect and disconnect parts so they could begin to see how computers were put together. As she recalled,

> We practiced troubleshooting problems by removing a piece, like the RAM or the hard drive, turning the computer on to see what happens, then putting the missing piece back to make the computer work again. Any problems we encountered along the way gave students hands-on experience with common computer issues, such as loose connections or circuit wires overheating.

By exposing the parts of the hardware they used, Thi and her students were able to dispel some of the mystery, and some of the fear, around how computers work.

Looking Closely at the Complex Nature of Pencils with Kindergarten Students at Emerson Elementary School

Looking closely can be practiced in many ways: Students might draw, make lists, or name the parts of a particular object; they might verbally describe intricacies or write descriptive observations. Any of these practices also cultivates a habit of slowing down. A great example of the development of this habit can be seen in Carla Aiello's kindergarten classroom at Emerson Elementary School, where she and her students spent almost an entire year closely examining pencils. What began as a simple exercise in naming the parts of this everyday object evolved into an in-depth exploration of each of the component properties of a pencil.

The project was conceived of by Carla in collaboration with Harriet Cohen, a retired educator from nearby Park Day School who began volunteering in Carla's classroom in 2013. Carla and Harriet chose to focus on pencils because they are accessible, everyday objects that reward deep exploration. While the project certainly featured all three of the capacities named earlier—looking closely, exploring complexity, and finding opportunity—here we highlight the many steps of this investigation that underscore the practice of looking closely. As Carla and Harriet explained, each student chose a pencil from a variety of styles and formats. They used the following prompts to launch the project: What is a pencil? What is it made of? What can you do with a pencil? Students were asked to think about what pencils are used for and to notice some commonalities and differences among them. They noticed that some pencils had letters and numbers; some had erasers and eraser clamps; some were multicolored and some were plain yellow.

The pencil project engaged students in a wide range of close-looking activities. For example, the students watched a "How Pencils Are Made" video,[2] they used pencil sharpeners to understand how they worked, they took apart and reassembled mechanical pencils, and they made pencils of their own. Students were also offered blank pencil journals and were invited to see what they could do with sticks of graphite. "They described how it felt to write and draw with graphite," Harriet explained, "how the graphite came off on their fingers and, in some cases, how easily it broke. When asked why wood was put around the graphite in a pencil, most students quickly agreed that it was to protect the graphite and to keep hands and papers clean."

As the pencil project evolved, Carla's students experienced many opportunities to explore the properties of pencils and ultimately to collaborate on a giant pencil sculpture that expressed how pencils could be used as powerful tools for communicating messages and that displayed each child's idea for how they could possibly use pencils to make the world a better place.

The unit was playful and engaging—and yielded multiple learning outcomes. Carla noticed her students investigating simple items in depth, developing a sensitivity to their design, and reflecting on their work. Carla watched as her students developed the ability to look closely and critically, hopeful in her anticipation that her students would "transfer their close looking skills to other parts of their life and other curriculum areas."

Exploring Complexity

Although the capacities of looking closely, exploring complexity, and finding opportunity were not designed to be enacted in a strict sequential order, it is hard to imagine exploring complexity without first looking closely. Much of the time, looking closely and exploring complexity are connected: To explore the complexity of an object or system, it is usually necessary to have first looked at it closely. Like looking closely, exploring the complexity of an object or system involves looking beyond what is immediately observable: It is to think about the relationships between the various parts of an object or system, to consider how the object or system is used (and by whom), and to develop a nuanced understanding of how it was made. Exploring complexity takes time and often requires drawing on multiple disciplines and sources of knowledge. It is about uncovering the layers of what it is one can see, and speculating about the mechanics of what one cannot see. The process of exploring complexity encourages critical thinking by probing the relationships between parts and wholes, understanding interactions and causality, and questioning the why, how, and for whom of the objects and systems one encounters. Beyond noticing materials and mechanics, exploring complexity further involves a sensitivity to the range of values, motivations, and priorities held by those who engage with an object or system, including an understanding of the politics and power structures associated with their functionality. Ultimately, exploring complexity involves moving beyond understanding an object as a static, discrete item to thinking about it in relation to the many dynamic and complex systems in which it participates.

Looking Closely and Exploring the Complexity of Electricity and Circuits with Third Grade Students at Park Day School

While Thi and her high school students were looking closely at computers and exploring their complexity, around the corner at Park Day School, third-grade teacher Renee Miller was embarking on her annual electricity and circuits unit. Having taught the unit before, Renee's typical curricular trajectory included first explaining to students how light bulbs work. But during her first year of working with Agency *by* Design, she changed her plan and instead began by asking her students to do some close looking (Figure 5.3). One student noticed that a piece of wire was soldered to the base of the bulb. Upon further examination, the student's friend noticed that in fact there were two places where the wire was soldered to the base of the bulb. The pair of students then tried to trace the wires inside the bulb to understand what they were connected to, which led to conjectures about why the wires were there. "Frustrated that they couldn't see all the parts," Renee explained, "they finally asked to break it open. I hadn't offered this as an option, but I knew it was where we were headed."

Driven by that initial observation, the students' curiosity led them to go deeper than their first look, to look again, and to look critically. Building on that

FIGURE 5.3: To better understand scientific principles behind light and electricity, a third-grade student in Renee Miller's class breaks down a light bulb into its individual elements.

curiosity—admittedly a bit nervously—Renee provided teams of students with a light bulb, a paper bag, a plastic bag, a smashing tool, gloves, and goggles. As students began to open their bulbs, Renee quickly saw the opportunities for learning. Students were making observations about a white powder coating, connections between wires and springs, electric coils, and putty. They began to question why the various parts of the light bulb were there and what function each had. The experience was illuminating for Renee as well: "The light bulb lesson always required a great deal of telling as teaching, and many students never really understood as I tried to explain what was happening on the inside of a light bulb," she said. But this time, "students constructed an understanding of the workings of an incandescent light bulb, and came away with one mental model of an electrical system."

This picture of practice illustrating how Renee's students explored the complexity of a light bulb offers a provocative glimpse into how looking closely at an object can provide an entry point into the nontransparent concept of electricity while inspiring students to make predictions and test hypotheses based on their observations.

Looking Closely and Exploring the Complexity of Telephones, Manufacturing, and Communication Systems with Eighth-Grade Students at East Bay School for Boys

Not far from Renee's third-grade classroom at the Park Day School, Kyle Metzner and Corrina Hui's eighth-grade students at East Bay School for Boys in Berkeley, California, were likewise engaged in the process of looking closely and exploring complexity. Kyle and Corrina's students were participating in a unit of cross-curricular inquiry on cellular phones: In math class they gained statistical skills by examining and comparing the true cost of phone plans; in history class they explored the external costs of cell phone production and consumption, including the human impact of labor practices and the environmental impact of electronic waste disposal; and in a class called "Work" they took analog and cell phones fully apart to consider how planned obsolescence manifests itself in phone design and choice of materials. The activity of deconstructing and looking closely at various phones provided an entry point into a quite sophisticated inquiry in which students were able to investigate issues of resource procurement, identify important manufacturing shifts (e.g., old phones are made to have replaceable parts; new phones are not), and notice trends in telephone design over the years.

For Kyle and Corrina's students, investigating the materials-to-waste life span of cell phones began with close looking and migrated beyond classroom walls. They created a public art piece about waste related to cell phone consumption. They interviewed people across generations to understand the history and evolution of telephones and technology, and they examined the many systems within which cell phone use can be situated. Students explored their own complex habits and relationships to their personal cell phone devices; they had an opportunity to meaningfully connect their learning experiences to their own lives by examining their personal decisions about cell phone plans and carriers. As Corrina explained:

> Students practiced media and financial literacy by analyzing cell phone provider advertising campaigns and promotions. They dug deeper by reading the fine print on the provider websites and on third-party reviews to identify the true costs and constraints. Students were excited by the results of their investigations and shocked by how misleading cell phone advertisements can be.

By exploring the complexity of cell phones in this multifaceted way, Kyle and Corrina's students no longer viewed the cell phones they used as isolated objects, but instead recognized the networks of interactions within which their cell phones were situated. They further came to understand that the decisions they made concerning their personal cell phone use have an effect on other elements and people participating in this complex system.

Finding Opportunity

Finding opportunity is about seeing the potential for building, tinkering, re/designing, or hacking. It is like the philosopher Maxine Greene's idea of imagining the world as if it could be otherwise,[3] along with having a proclivity toward action. Of the three capacities, finding opportunity is most directly linked to agency because it is about pursuing change in one's world. Finding opportunity builds on looking closely and exploring complexity because often it is in doing these things—closely examining objects and systems and exploring their complexities—that the possibility for change becomes visible. In other words, finding opportunity builds on an examination of how things work, why they work the way they do, and how they could be made to work otherwise.

Finding opportunity can start with an exploration of materials, as Jenny Ernst's sixth-graders at Park Day School did, when Jenny asked them to think critically about the properties of Mylar and then imagine where else that material might be useful. It can also start with an exploration of user needs and available resources, as Jenny's fellow teacher Alex Kane at Park Day School did, when he challenged his fifth-grade students to redesign their classroom to promote movement and enhance learning, as shown in Figure 5.4. Noticing how much time students spent sitting, Alex found an opportunity to redesign their learning environment and invited his students to further investigate that opportunity. "The physical space of a classroom is a system," he recalled, "complete with numerous parts that can be understood,

Photo by Jeanine Harmon.

FIGURE 5.4: Students in Alex Kane's fifth-grade class redesign their classroom workspace, starting with the furniture, after analyzing the benefits of student movement on the brain and overall health.

analyzed, and thoughtfully modified. That system needs to be pulled apart and my classroom needed to be redesigned to better suit the needs of my students. Who better to do that than the students themselves?"

This theme of redesigning learning environments was of special interest to the group of Oakland educators who worked with Agency *by* Design, particularly in terms of how the design of teaching and learning environments could best support maker-centered learning. The following two pictures of practice show how educators found ways to bring this theme to life.

During the second year of the Agency *by* Design research initiative, our teacher partners in Oakland collaborated with architect and educator David Stephen. The goal of this collaboration was to find opportunities at each school for enabling maker-centered learning experiences while activating maker-empowered students and teachers. David engaged each school in conversation about the following questions:

- What kinds of learning environments, spaces, and spatial characteristics best support design and maker-centered thinking and learning?

- How can teachers and students reenvision their school facilities as more maker-centered environments?

- How can design and maker-centered thinking and learning activate agency in students and teachers and influence the ways they plan and interact with their physical environments?

- What effect do spaces, adjacencies, and amenities that strive to facilitate design and maker-centered thinking and learning have on the life of a school?

Finding opportunity to integrate maker-centered thinking and learning into the pattern of daily life in these schools was about first understanding their respective climates, cultures, people, and needs. There was no blueprint to follow; conceiving a maker area that followed a preordained plan would not have met the needs of each community. It was important to include strategies for no- and low-cost, short- and long-term facility changes that promoted maker-centered thinking and learning. At each school, a maker campus plan responded to the strengths, challenges, goals, and opportunities afforded by each site. Here are two examples of these collaborations between architect and educators.

Engaging in a Library Redesign at Oakland International High School

At Oakland International High School, David worked with several teachers to facilitate student design projects for developing their maker campus (Figure 5.5). As David explained, students "had the opportunity to not only identify spaces and systems within the school that they would like to redesign, but also to actually implement their ideas and physically transform their campus."

Art teacher Brooke Toczylowski, for instance, had initiated a library redesign project with an afterschool group made up of students and teachers. Brooke

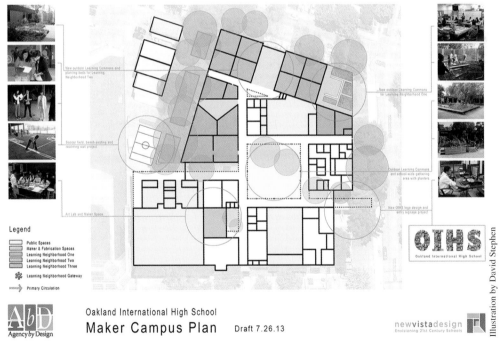

FIGURE 5.5: The proposed design for a maker campus at Oakland International High School.

explained that, when the project began, "I expected to create a formalized design plan of what we would do with the library and then I imagined it happening, swiftly. I imagined easy consensus, and lots of elbow grease." What she had not expected was the "barrage of changes they wanted to make. It was like, 'Finally! Someone asked our opinion!'" Though eager to dive into the work, Brooke felt that spending ample time in the design phase really connected to the needs of her community. As she watched a recording of a meeting among a few students, a teacher, and a security guard, she noted a key moment when the security guard and one of the students made a personal connection. "In this moment I could see the brainstorming process having powerful effects. Not only were we building community by uniting as designers making decisions together, but this moment was shifting students' perceptions of how they interact with the space and the people within it."

For the students at Oakland International High School, developing a sensitivity to design was supported by all three maker capacities: the students looked closely at the components of their library; they explored complexity by considering the needs and interests of the various people who used the space; and, most germane to a discussion of finding opportunity, they used what they had learned about the library's form and function to find opportunities to make it more user friendly, more efficient, and more accessible to students and teachers.

Mapping a Maker Campus at Claremont Middle School

Claremont Middle School is a socioeconomically and ethnically diverse public school in Oakland that serves Grades 6–8. When David Stephen began working with this school, an initial meeting with school staff revealed the importance they placed on providing students with a structured and safe school facility. Accordingly, several goals of the partnership were articulated: to build a community and culture of trust and collaboration; to make the school more user friendly; and to celebrate student thinking and learning. In planning meetings, David explained that it was important that teachers and students be "encouraged and challenged to customize their classrooms and hallways, and as a result, take greater ownership of the school and responsibility for making sure that it was well maintained and respected."

David worked particularly closely with Claremont Middle School design thinking and making educator Maite Barloga. Their partnership led to a series of student-inspired, student-directed, and student-implemented activities. Echoing what David learned through staff meetings, Maite explained that she wanted her students to be the ones taking ownership over their space to transform it into a place where they felt safe, inspired, and in control. She started the project by asking her students to get really familiar with their learning spaces. Working in small design teams, students spent several days looking closely at the school environment, analyzing it, revisiting their initial observations, sketching, and looking again. They observed hallway movements and flow of traffic; they explored classrooms and outdoor spaces and noticed what worked and what did not. They mapped out their campus and created three-dimensional models of rooms and hallways and entire wings of the school. As a result of these observations and activities, they noticed a lack of signage in the school, a lack of identity, and a lack of community. Encouraged by David and Maite, the students found opportunity to address these issues by designing prototypes, redesigning signage, and adding display cases for celebrating student learning. Their work built firmly on their earlier efforts to examine and understand the design components of their school and the complex nature of the needs and interests of the people who used its hallways and classrooms each day.

Tools and Techniques for Supporting Maker-Centered Thinking and Learning

The stories we have told in this chapter thus far show a variety of ways in which teachers have cultivated the three primary capacities that support maker empowerment—looking closely, exploring complexity, and finding opportunity. Although practices like the ones described previously lay a great foundation for developing these capacities, it is important to keep in mind the broader goal of maker empowerment, which is to encourage students to be sensitive to the design dimensions of their worlds and empowered to effect change—even when structured lessons are not there to cue them to do so. This presents a bit of a conundrum: Given the fact that students are receiving structured instruction—indeed, that is what school-based learning is mainly about—how can their learning experiences be designed to foster dispositional behavior beyond the context in which instruction is delivered?

Dispositional Development and Thinking Routines

One of the recurring themes of this book is that maker empowerment is a dispositional outcome. Here it is worth recalling again Project Zero's concept of thinking dispositions. In previous chapters we have described the research that led to the view that dispositional behavior is comprised of three elements—ability, inclination, and sensitivity—and underscored the important finding that sensitivity to opportunity is a key developmental bottleneck: In other words, people often do not activate dispositional behavior because they simply do not notice opportunities to do so. There is no magic bullet method to address the issue of sensitivity, but it helps to remember that dispositions, by definition, are habits of mind—tendencies toward regular patterns of behavior that people develop like any other habit, by regularly engaging in certain forms of behavior until those behaviors become routine.

Project Zero researchers have leveraged the idea of routine behavior and developed a set of practices called thinking routines, which are short, engaging, two- or three-step patterns of intellectual behavior that are highly transferable across contexts. They are designed to be easy to use, easy to remember, easy to transfer, and vividly effective when used on a wide variety of topics. The idea is that when classroom instruction includes the frequent use of thinking routines across a range of subjects and contexts, students will become habituated to using these routines as a matter of course. In other words, they will develop dispositions related to the patterns of thinking the routines promote. Since the early 1990s, the concept of thinking routines has been generative for Project Zero. As a result, thinking routines have become central to several recent Project Zero research initiatives, including Visible Thinking, Artful Thinking, and Cultures of Thinking.[4]

Developing Thinking Routines to Support a Sensitivity to Design

Given this backdrop, it was natural for the Agency *by* Design team to wonder what it would be like to develop thinking routines to support the dispositional concept of maker empowerment. Specifically, we wondered what kinds of thinking routines we could borrow from other Project Zero initiatives, or develop ourselves, that would cultivate the three primary maker capacities: looking closely, exploring complexity, and finding opportunity? The question captivated us, and over the course of the project we worked closely with our teacher partners to explore and pilot-test several thinking routines. Eventually we settled on four signature thinking routines. Each one encourages one or more of the three maker capacities described in our pedagogical framework—and all of them can be used across contexts and subjects. In the following sections we describe each of these four thinking routines in turn, including a brief version of each. Appendix B provides more complete description of the routines, along with helpful tips (these thinking routines can also be found on the Agency *by* Design website: www.agencybydesign.org).

Parts, Purposes, Complexities

If there is a core Agency *by* Design thinking routine—a routine that cultivates the slow looking that is so fundamental to developing a sensitivity to design—it is

---

Parts, Purposes, Complexities

Choose an object or system and ask:

What are its **parts**?

What are its various pieces or components?

What are its **purposes**?

What are the purposes for each of these parts?

What are its **complexities**?

How is it complicated in its parts and purposes, the relationship between the two, or in other ways?

Parts, Purposes, Complexities. This is the first thinking routine our teacher partners used with their students, and, at this writing, it is still the most widely used of all the Agency *by* Design thinking routines.

Inspired by the ideas presented in David Perkins's book, *Knowledge as Design,*[5] this thinking routine was originally developed as a part of the Artful Thinking initiative at Project Zero.[6] Adopted for the maker-centered classroom, the Parts, Purposes, Complexities thinking routine is designed to help students slow down and look closely at an object or system, as in Figure 5.6. As Agency *by* Design researcher Shari Tishman has noted in the past, engaging in the process of slow looking has the potential to support the maker capacities of looking closely and exploring complexity:

> *Closely examining everyday objects sparks students' curiosity and leads to increasingly complex thinking. . . . You'll find that once students start generating observations and ideas about an object, it's hard to get them to stop. That's because looking carefully at something and trying to discern its features is a form of cognition with an intrinsically rewarding feedback loop. The more you look, the more you see; the more you see the more interesting the object becomes.*[7]

To help illustrate what the Parts, Purposes, Complexities thinking routine looks like in action, picture an apple pie. That's right. Apple pie. Not the popular Raspberry Pi microprocessor. Apple pie—the iconic dessert served in roadside diners across the United States. Now an apple pie may not seem like a typical built object, but of course apple pies are carefully crafted, designed, and redesigned by people in an intentional way. Apple pies are systems, made up of subsystems, which are situated within broader supersystems. In this way, baking an apple pie can be—and should be—considered just as much of a maker endeavor as building a quad-copter, engineering a robot—or programming a Raspberry Pi. As it happens, our teacher partners in Oakland feel the same way, and we have enjoyed watching them use an apple pie as a focal point for the Parts, Purposes, Complexities thinking routine. What follows is an example of how this exercise might play out.

The first question in the routine asks, What are its parts? By looking closely at an apple pie, students begin by naming all the parts they initially see. At first glance,

Photo by Jeanine Harmon.

FIGURE 5.6: A student in the woodworking shop looking closely while setting up the work space.

they may just notice two parts: the crust on the outside, and the apples on the inside. But on closer inspection, more details emerge. They may notice, for example, that there are slits cut into the top of the piecrust and that the crust is bumpy around the edges of the pie. If students cut a slice of the pie and look yet more closely, they may notice that there is a bottom crust and an upper crust—and a gooey middle. Taking a bite, they will notice even more. Certainly, they will taste apples, but they may also taste cinnamon and the tang of lemon as well. Of course, if the students were to watch someone make an apple pie, they would see the dough that forms the crust is made of many parts, including flour, sugar, salt, and butter. The filling of the apple pie is made of even more parts. Yes, there are the apples and the cinnamon and lemon that they tasted on first bite, but there are also, butter, sugar, and nutmeg in the mix as well.

Having noticed the many parts of an apple pie, students address the second question of the thinking routine, What are the purposes?, by considering the purposes of the parts they noticed. For example, they may focus on the slits in the piecrust and come to understand that they are there to allow steam to be released from the inside of the pie as it cooks in the oven. They may come to understand that the bumpy bits around the edges of the piecrust are there to give the apple pie its classic crenulated look but also to pinch the bottom crust and the upper crust together through a process called fluting.

Now that students have considered the parts and purposes of the various elements of the apple pie, they turn to the third question in the routine, What are its complexities?, and think about how the various parts of the pie come together in ways that are complex. Although students may not use the language of systems thinking, right away they may notice that an apple pie is a system composed of two primary subsystems: the outer crusts and the inner filling. Each of these subsystems is composed of parts that all have specific purposes and which all come together in ways that are complex. Taking a closer look at the filling of an apple pie, students may come to understand that apples, cinnamon, nutmeg, lemon juice, sugar, and salt may just seem like a heap of stuff on their own, but when combined in particular amounts and prepared in a particular way each of these parts come together in a complex—and yummy—way.

By using the Parts, Purposes, Complexities thinking routine, young people learn that something as seemingly simple as an apple pie is actually a complex system. They also learn, as we suggested earlier, that the closer they look at something the more there is to see, and the more they see, the more interesting the thing becomes. This happens not just with apple pies, of course. The Parts, Purposes, Complexities thinking routine can be used with a wide variety of objects and systems. In fact, we have seen this thinking routine used fruitfully on all manner of things, from mechanical tools, small appliances, and light electronics to poems, lunch lines, and pencils.

Parts, People, Interactions

A second Agency by Design thinking routine is called *Parts, People, Interactions*. Like Parts, Purposes, Complexities, this routine is designed to support the maker

Parts, People, Interactions

Identify a system and ask:

What are the **parts** of the system?

Who are the **people** connected to the system?

How do the people in the system **interact** with each other and with the parts of the system?

How does a change in one element of the system affect the various parts and people connected to the system?

capacities of looking closely and exploring complexity. The Parts, People, Interactions thinking routine can be used on its own, or as a follow-up to Parts, Purposes, Complexities. Either way, it encourages students to explore the complexity of systems and, in particular, the multiple and complex ways people participate in systems.

To get a feel for the kind of thinking this routine is meant to encourage, let's return again to the example of an apple pie. In the foregoing section, we saw how students were able to look closely at an apple pie to understand it as a complex system composed of subsystems. We also hinted that an apple pie can be situated within greater supersystems. At Emerson Elementary School in Oakland, California, Carla Aiello and her kindergarten students did just that. Starting with the basic concept of an apple pie, Carla and her students developed systems maps that placed apple pies within various systems. In one systems map, Carla's students sketched out an apple's journey from its origins in an orchard to its end state as an apple pie, as shown in Figure 5.7. Along the way, her students noted the various parts of the system: apples, apple trees, ladders, baskets, produce trucks, grocery stores, ovens, and houses. They also considered the various people who participate in this system: apple growers, apple pickers, families who visit apple orchards to go apple picking, truck drivers who deliver apples to grocery stores, produce clerks, cashiers, and then the people who bake apple pies—including the young people themselves (with the help of their parents, of course). Using multidirectional

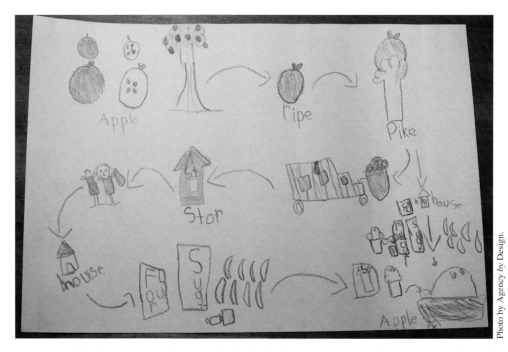

FIGURE 5.7: Kindergarten students in Carla Aiello's class map out the parts, people, and interactions associated with the system of making an apple pie.

arrows and other drawing techniques, the students further indicated how the various people within this system interact with one another and with the various parts of the system.

In this particular example, Carla's young students did not explicitly use the Parts, People, and Interactions thinking routine. In fact, we had not developed it yet! Instead, the systems maps generated by Carla's kindergarten students—as well as those developed by students in her colleagues' classrooms—helped us understand how focusing on parts, people, and interactions can help learners discover and explore the complexity of systems. Thus, building on the work of Carla and her colleagues, the Parts, People, Interactions thinking routine was developed. Since then, it has been used in many settings to help students understand the various— and sometimes conflicting—perspectives of the many people who participate in a particular system.

A particularly interesting recent example comes from Aaron Vanderwerff at Light-house Community Charter School. Following a Black Lives Matter protest that stopped traffic on the Bay Bridge (which connects Oakland to San Francisco) on Martin Luther King Day, Aaron and his students used this thinking routine to explore the protest as a system, including the various parts of the protest, the multiple people involved and affected by the protest, and the ways the different people interacted with one another and each part of the system.

In its focus on people, the Parts, People, Interactions thinking routine shares some similarities with the popular concept of *user-centered design* associated with various protocols for design thinking,[8] which imagines a designed system from the perspective of a user at the center of it. But some limitations to a user-centered design perspective are worth pointing out. For example, as Kevin Slavin noted in a recent article titled "Design as Participation," a user-centered approach to design limits the degree to which designers (or makers) can understand their roles in a given system—or to even understand the greater complexity of the system itself. As Slavin commented, "When designers center around the user, where do the needs and desires of the other actors in the system go? The lens of the user obscures the view of the ecosystems it affects."[9] Moving away from the user–designer approach, Slavin advocates instead for a more participatory approach to making and design. "Designing for participation is different than designing for use,"[10] he argued. From this perspective, the maker or designer becomes an engaged participant in the built environment, as opposed to a removed agent wielding his or her external power upon that environment. "Some contemporary work suggests that we are not only designing for participation," Slavin has argued, "but that design is a fundamentally participatory act. . . . This is design as an activity that doesn't place the designer *or* the user in the center."[11]

In the spirit of Slavin's remarks, the Parts, People, Interactions thinking routine attempts to stretch beyond placing the user solely at the center of a system, and instead considers the multiple roles various people might play within a system. For example, we have seen the Parts, People, and Interactions thinking routine applied to topics such as product design, traffic patterns, school lunch lines, local bike paths, and even the practice of trick or treating.

Think, Feel, Care

A third Agency *by* Design thinking routine is called *Think, Feel, Care*. The purpose of this thinking routine is to encourage students to imaginatively envision the roles various stakeholders play within a system. Here, once again, it is helpful to think about the example of apple pie. Recall the systems maps Carla's kindergarteners made that showed the parts, people, and interactions they associated with an apple-pie-making system. Using the Think, Feel, Care thinking routine, Carla's students might try to imagine the perspective of the truck driver who delivers the apples to the bakery. They might try to envision the thoughts and concerns of the apple farmers and their families. Perhaps they may try to imagine the experience of the person purchasing the pie, or the perspective of the bakery workers who do the cleaning up. Imaginatively envisioning any of these perspectives will likely deepen their understanding on the larger pie-making system.

The Think, Feel, Care thinking routine leverages the natural human capacity for empathy by encouraging students to imagine the experience of people other than themselves. But it is important to remember that empathy is a powerful cognitive tool that has its perils and must be exercised carefully. First of all, as a matter of respect, none of us can truly claim to know how another person feels: Empathy can

---

Think, Feel, Care

Step inside a system:

Choose a variety of people within a system and then step inside each person's point of view. As you think about what you know about the system, consider what each person might think, feel, and care about:

Think: How does this person understand this system and their role within it?

Feel: What is this person's emotional response to the system and to their position within it?

Care: What are this person's values, priorities, or motivations with regard to the system? What is important to this person?

---

illuminate the kinds of thoughts and feelings and concerns someone else might have, but one must always regard these insights as suggestions only, and resist being overly certain. Further, as generous as students' imaginations can sometimes be, they are shaped (and often limited) by their own experiences. One simply cannot know the thoughts or feelings of people whose experiences are hugely different from his or her own, and to assume one can is a mark of disrespect. Moreover, lack of information about someone else's viewpoint can lead to overgeneralization and stereotype, no matter how well-intentioned the effort. As a poignant example of this, recall the story we told earlier about the students at East Bay School for Boys who wanted to make something to help the homeless residents of their neighborhood. They began to design hooks for the homeless that they thought would be helpful, but it was not until they actually interviewed some homeless people and learned firsthand about their needs that they were able to envision the kind of functionality the hooks truly needed—specifically to hold items and keep clothes dry in the shower area at the local shelter—not to hook bags onto shopping carts as the young students had initially thought.

Imagine If . . .

The fourth Agency *by* Design thinking routine is *Imagine if . . . .* This routine was designed to specifically target the maker capacity of finding opportunity. Its purpose is to encourage students to consider how objects and systems might be designed—or redesigned—in positive ways. But it is not merely an open-ended

---

Imagine If . . .

Choose an object or system:

Consider the parts, purposes, and people who interact with your object or system, and then ask:

In what ways could it be made to be more **effective?**

In what ways could it be made to be more **efficient?**

In what ways could it be made to be more **ethical?**

In what ways could it be made to be more **beautiful?**

brainstorming activity. Rather, it offers concrete criteria for envisioning improvement. Specifically, it encourages young people to consider how the designed dimensions of their worlds can be made more effective, more efficient, more ethical, or more beautiful.

To share a sense of what it is like to use this thinking routine, we return one final time to Carla's kindergarten students. As part of their discussion with Carla, students considered the implications of using apples from a grocery store versus using apples hand-picked from a local orchard. If they were to use the Imagine if . . . thinking routine, perhaps they would expand on their reflections and envision making an apple pie more beautiful, for example by changing the way it looks, tastes, or smells. Perhaps the kindergarteners would focus on equity and would imagine how to make the pie easier to share, for example by marking the crust before baking so the pie can be more easily cut into eight equal pieces once it is done. Eventually, the kindergartners may broaden their thinking and use the Imagine if . . . routine to think about pie making at the systems level. For example, perhaps the students want to make apple farming more organic and therefore envision changes in the process of growing apples. Perhaps they want to make the apple-picking system more efficient, and therefore consider how to make better apple-picking devices. Maybe they want to make the system more fun, and therefore consider how to bring a carnival atmosphere to the apple-picking process. Whatever they do, the hope is that by using the routine regularly—on apples pies and beyond—they build their capacity to become alert to opportunities to shape—or reshape—their worlds.

These four thinking routines have been designed to be nonsequential yet synergistic. Each routine can be used solo, or in combination with the others, and all four thinking routines have been designed to support the development of the maker capacities described earlier in this chapter—looking closely, exploring complexity, and finding opportunity, as in Figure 5.8. It is also important to remember that this suite of thinking routines is not meant to exist as a set of stand-alone activities but rather as a means to develop habits of mind by routinizing particular ways of thinking. In other words, these

Photo by Brad Gentile.

FIGURE 5.8: Students at Propel McKeesport School in Pittsburgh begin to engage with the Agency *by* Design maker capacities by documenting the parts, purposes, and complexities of their balloon car prototypes.

thinking routines—like all thinking routines—are meant to be repeated over and over again until they become a way of seeing the world.

Zooming back to the big picture, this chapter has presented a framework for instructional practice that is a capstone to the story of maker-centered learning that this book has endeavored to tell. In essence, the story is this: We believe that one of the fundamental goals of maker-centered learning is what the Agency *by* Design team has termed *maker empowerment*. We have defined maker empowerment as a dispositional outcome and have argued that one of the most effective ways to cultivate this way of seeing and being in the world is by helping students develop a sensitivity to design. Students will feel empowered to bring about change in the world through making by first coming to notice that many of the objects and systems they encounter are designs—designs that can be hacked, tweaked, reenvisioned, and reinvented. This sensitivity to design is supported by three maker capacities: the capacity to look closely at objects and systems, the capacity to explore the ways in which they are complex, and the capacity to find opportunities to change them. We offer this framework as a contribution to the emergent domain of maker-centered learning, and we hope it will be a useful addition to any maker educators' already well-stocked instructional toolkit.

Conclusion

The practice of making has been around for at least as long as *Homo sapiens* have had opposable thumbs. Throughout history, making has been a means not only of surviving but also of communicating, celebrating, reflecting, problem solving, influencing ideas, and inventing new ways of engaging with the world. Many programs in schools reflect this multiplicity of purposes: from vocational schools that prepare the next generation of carpenters and auto mechanics to arts education programs that encourage self-expression through the visual, performing, literary, and media arts, the K–12 curriculum has been endorsing hands-on and project-based learning for decades. And though many arts, design, and shop class programming in schools continue to be under fiscal fire, the resurgence in making that surfaced in the early 2000s brought with it renewed emphasis on the importance of making in schools.

Though it shares many similarities with traditional arts education and shop classes, with its focus on collaboration, sharing and learning from others, experimentation and iterative processes, and interdisciplinary thinking, the *making* at the heart of this resurgence is also unique in many ways.

In this book we have positioned the resurgence of making as an opportunity to help young people activate their sense of agency, to view the world through a systems lens, and to develop a sense of maker empowerment. As we learned from the many maker educators and thought leaders we have spoken with, maker-centered learning is not merely about acquiring making and discipline-specific knowledge and skills, it is also, and perhaps more importantly, about building character, gaining creative confidence, being resourceful and courageous. Through our work on the Agency *by* Design project we have come to understand that the biggest aspiration for maker-centered learning is to develop a sensitivity to the designed dimensions of one's world, to see that world as malleable, and ultimately to believe in one's capacity to shape that world through building, tinkering, re/designing, or hacking.

Our work with the many educators we interviewed, paired with our Oakland-based teacher partners, has helped us come to understand that the maker capacities of looking closely, exploring complexity, and finding opportunity are central to developing a sensitivity to design, and are therefore elemental to our framework for maker-centered learning (Figure C.1). Once again, thanks to our collaboration with our Oakland-based teacher partners, we have further developed the suite of

Photo by Jeanine Harmon.

FIGURE C.I: A young student fully engages all three maker capacities while working through a carpentry project.

thinking routines presented in Chapter Five to serves as tools to support the maker capacities of looking closely, exploring complexity, and finding opportunity.

Throughout this book we have argued that maker empowerment—agency seen through the lens of making—is dispositional in nature. We believe that this disposition—and the maker capacities that support it—can be fostered through the variety of learning that takes place both in and outside of the maker-centered classroom. To that end, we have explored the moves educators make to equip their students with a sensitivity to design and foster maker empowerment. Maker-centered learning, according to the passionate educators we encountered, looks different from many traditional classrooms: knowledge, information, and expertise moves between student, teacher, community members, and materials; teaching and learning is distributed; the physical and social environment is flexible and follows learning goals; and ideas flow and build on each other, generated by the collective. To engender maker-empowered young people, educators make intentional decisions across these fronts, including how to organize and display materials, how to encourage students to figure out problems for themselves, how to help them feel comfortable with the unknown, and being willing to experiment and explore.

Although we have learned a great deal throughout our exploration of maker-centered learning, which we have endeavored to share throughout this book, we have also arrived at this stage in our work with several questions and puzzles concerning various aspects of the maker-centered landscape.

Maker-Centered Learning: Challenges and Puzzles

Undoubtedly there is great enthusiasm around incorporating maker-centered practices into education. Yet despite the recognized benefits and outcomes associated with this work, there are very real hurdles to overcome. We share the excitement that has bubbled to the surface around the potential of maker-centered learning, but we are also deeply aware of some hard questions it raises—questions about the ethics of maker-centered practice, issues of access and equity, and the sustainability of maker-centered programs and curricula.

Considering the Ethical Dimensions of Maker-Centered Learning

When considering the intersections of ethics and maker-centered learning, one has to look no further than the 3-D printer to see potential dilemmas. In 2013, a Texas-based nonprofit organization named Defense Distributed announced they would be making downloadable and publicly accessible design files for a single-shot handgun. Perhaps not surprisingly, the U.S. State Department responded by demanding the company—whose advertised charge is to "collaboratively produce, publish, and distribute to the public without charge information and knowledge related to the digital manufacture of arms"—remove the files from their site.[1] Defense Distributed complied, but not before the plans were downloaded over 100,000 times. Just a year before, the Wiki Weapon Project, launched by Defense Distributed, released plans for the working parts of an AR-15 assault rifle. These designs were subsequently hosted on Thingiverse, the popular website that serves the maker community. Thingiverse soon pulled the rifle design from its website but, once again, not before hundreds of successful downloads.

At the time, *Wired* magazine posted an article raising concerns for the implications of 3-D printed weapons. Highlighting a post from the firearm resource website AR15.com, the article described a thread that reveals a widespread "culture of gun fandom." As the *Wired* article noted:

> There are guns with Star Wars insignia, guns with jokes about the zombie apocalypse, pink guns, minimalist machined guns, and baroque monsters covered in bells and whistles and laser sights. Each one was lovingly built and detailed with the same care given to modding a hot rod, custom-building a PC, or creating a 3-D printed Yoda head.[2]

Of course, 3-D printing gun parts does not necessarily result in destructive behavior. Further, it certainly is not the only industry whose fans are also participants in the maker community. Interest in lock picking, making homemade gun powder and improvised explosive devices, affixing cameras to quadcopters, developing invasive bots and malware, and using 3-D bioprinters to make human organs all surface moral, ethical, and legal implications of maker-centered culture.

In all of these examples, the potential for harm is significant. Maker educators, like any educators, sometimes have hard choices to make. We believe that if the goal of teaching and learning in the maker-centered classroom is to empower young people to shape their worlds, then educators in those spaces have a responsibility to discuss the ethics of making with their students, and to actively intervene if either the product, process, or intention of making runs a serious risk of bringing harm into the world.[3]

Just as we have encouraged educators to slow down their practice and to encourage students to look closely and explore the complexity of the designed dimensions of their worlds, so too do we encourage maker educators to find the opportunities to discuss with their students issues of ethics, emphasizing that like any tool, the empowerment and sense of *I can do that* which students gain from their experiences in the maker-centered classroom must be used as a tool for good.

Equity and Access in the Maker-Centered Classroom

Another set of questions regarding maker-centered learning concerns equity: Who is maker-centered learning for? Who does it spotlight and favor? Who are the champions and beneficiaries? Indeed, not long after the flurry of enthusiasm surrounding maker-centered learning began, important concerns focused on issues of access and equity soon rose to the surface. "Are the maker movement and maker-centered learning really as warm and welcoming as they claim to be?" some began to ask—and rightly so.

Nestled among the glow of LED lights and the buzz of drones, a small display within the education tent at the 2015 Bay Area Maker Faire directly addressed this question. Within this display, a small placard reported statistics from the 2014 Bay Area Maker Faire: 97% of attendees held college degrees, the median household income of attendees was a comfortable $130,000, and 70% of attendees were male. The provocative placard may not have cited its sources, but a quick, unscientific scan of the crowd at the 2015 Bay Area Maker Faire seemed to confirm the 2014 statistics. Happily, the display did not stop there. Next to the placard were two boards soliciting suggestions to address these issues. One read "make making more accessible to . . ." and the other read "make making more accessible by . . ." Both were filled with crowd-sourced suggestions penciled on multi-colored Post-it Notes.

Though we cannot fully know the true intentions of the makers who put together this display, we would like to think that their goals were not merely to raise the important question of how can we make the maker movement and maker-centered learning more accessible to a broader and more socially and culturally diverse population of young people and adults? Rather, we think it was to take a stance, make a demand, and raise a challenge: We must make the maker movement and maker-centered learning more accessible to a broader and more socially and culturally diverse population of young people and adults.

As community- and school-based maker-centered learning has gained momentum, some educators and researchers have decried the maker movement's inherent biases. The practices of the maker movement, they note, preference and celebrate white, middle-class boys and men. Further, some have argued that the type of making typically represented—robots, electronics, and rocketry—favors the interests of young, white boys while overlooking the interests of young girls and children of color.[4]

These critiques center on issues of access and equity. Access quite plainly means what it suggests: make making more easily accessible to a broader swath of young people and adults. Access, in this sense, means eliminating the barriers to entry. But just making making experiences more accessible to a more diverse population of young people does not mean that those experiences become more equitable. Even if maker-centered learning were to become universally accessible, that universal access would do little to address the fact that some people arrive at a makerspace or in the maker-centered classroom more advantaged or disadvantaged than others. Issues of advantage stretch beyond the domain of access and into the domain of equity.

As Mindy Kornhaber and her colleagues have noted, to move beyond the equal view that access suggests we must embrace more equalizing and expansive views of equity.[5] In this regard, equity concerns itself with providing greater resources and support to disadvantaged individuals than to their more privileged peers. Different from access, Shirin Vossoughi and her colleagues have noted that "equity lies in the how of teaching and learning."[6] In a paper presented at the 2013 FabLearn conference in Stanford, California, these researchers have suggested that in order to make making and tinkering experiences more equitable, maker educators must consider how they design their learning environments, how they use instructional language, and how they make cultural and historical connections that make making more relevant and meaningful for a broader array of learners. We think this emphasis on the learning dimensions of making is exactly right (Figure C.2).

Photo by Melissa Rivard.

FIGURE C.2: Exploration and experimentation in the maker-centered classroom can be made more accessible and equitable through the careful planning and facilitation of maker educators.

Supporting and Sustaining Maker-Centered Practice

A third challenge related to maker-centered learning is sustaining its presence in the curriculum beyond the initial honeymoon of interest and enthusiasm that is taking place right now. As we learned through our review of literature, interviews with maker-educators, and site visits to schools and organizations across the country, maker-centered learning quite often occupies a precarious space in the structure and curriculum of schools—especially, as noted above, in public and traditional schools. This is generally true of any new program introduced into the entrenched ecosystem of a school, but in the case of maker-centered learning, the problem may be exacerbated by the fact that maker-centered learning is not yet a formal discipline and does not have the backing of a professional and organized network.[7]

Often, a school's response to the challenge of integrating a new program is to offer faculty and staff professional development: In the case of maker-centered learning this might take the form of a workshop on maker-centered learning or a field trip to a successful maker-integration site or makerspace. Granted, the Agency *by Design* team members has taught their fair share of professional development workshops about thinking and learning in the maker-centered classroom, and in truth we have found that presenting workshops can be a quite effective way to share big ideas and core practices. But to sustain practice beyond an initial introduction to ideas, it is important to develop a cadre of educators who learn together, question together, engage in deep thinking together, and can then advocate for programs and positions feeling both confident and supported.

The power of creating a space where educators can come together to do these things was made visible to us by our Oakland-based teacher partners. Through the adult learning community they created, we saw how they established a space to test ideas and to explore uncharted territory. It was a space for educators new to maker-centered learning to share theories and puzzles, to build knowledge and confidence together. It was a space for researchers and teachers to experiment together, to pilot-test thinking routines, and to look closely at student work. And perhaps most importantly for the community, it provided an opportunity for educators to come together from different schools to share stories and strategies across schools that were physically proximate though demographically disparate.

Cultivating maker empowerment is not just a student outcome; it is important for educators to feel maker-empowered as well. Building on the community initially created in Oakland, several of the educators we worked with went on to exercise their sense of empowerment in different ways: forming a unified voice to advocate for positions and programs; leveraging resources in the community; integrating maker-centered teaching in curricula for which it is not explicitly designed or supported; organizing local maker educator meet-ups; facilitating maker empowerment workshops for other educators; and embracing the notion of teacher as learner. Perhaps most rewarding, we witnessed educators coalesce into a community of inquiry-driven, confident, risk-taking designers of their own maker-related teaching and learning experiences.

Looking Ahead: The Future of Maker-Centered Learning

What does the future hold for maker-centered learning? As the foregoing sections make clear, there is important work to be done on several fronts: ethical questions about making and learning need to be considered honestly and carefully; issues of equity and access need to be energetically addressed, as do the challenges of sustaining maker-centered learning initiatives in schools and creating communities of educators to support them. In addition to these challenges, we want to point to another very important one: If maker-centered learning is to become more than a passing trend, it is essential to develop assessment and documentation strategies that illustrate and support the educational outcomes associated with this work.

The challenge of measuring maker empowerment is tricky. The central argument of this book has been that the core educational outcomes of maker-centered learning concern the development of agency and character. These are broad dispositional outcomes, and measuring them—indeed even documenting them—is a very different enterprise than measuring, say, science, technology, engineering, and mathematics (STEM) skills using pre- and post-tests.

There is already noteworthy work being done in the area of maker assessments across the country. Two examples include the Open Portfolio Project, a collaboration between the Maker Education Initiative and Indiana University's Creativity

Lab, that is engaged in an effort to develop common practices for maker portfolios. Another example comes from the work of Tiffany Tseng at the Lifelong Kinder-garten Group at MIT's Media Lab. Here, Tiffany and her colleagues have been cre-ating documentation tools to capture making and design work in process. The Agency *by* Design team itself hopes to continue to work on the challenge of assessment, specifically by developing documentation and assessment strategies related to the three maker capacities that comprise the Agency *by* Design frame-work—looking closely, exploring complexity, and finding opportunity.

One of the most important aspects of developing documentation and assessment strategies for any type of learning is the idea of making thinking and learning visible. Researchers at Project Zero have long been interested in the topics of visible thinking and visible learning.[8] From the perspective of the Visible Thinking research team, visible thinking is defined as "any kind of observable representation that documents and supports the development of an individual's or group's ongoing thoughts, questions, reasons, and reflections."[9] We believe that by using the afore-mentioned thinking routines, it may be possible to make the variety of thinking that takes place in the maker-centered classroom visible.

When students are able to see external representations of their thinking as it unfolds, several important things happen. First of all, each individual student sees how his or her ideas contribute to a larger whole. For example, in using the Parts, Purposes, Complexities thinking routine, a teacher might keep evolving lists on the board of students' ideas and observations. Each time a student mentions a part, it gets written down—likewise, when a student mentions a purpose, and so on.

Another important thing that happens when the unfolding of students' thinking is made visible is that students are able to see that knowledge-building is an evolv-ing, dynamic process. Indeed, the physical artifacts of visible thinking—lists, maps, diagrams, sketches—can often be messy. Ideas get scribbled in, crossed out, moved around. Lines are drawn to show linkages; key thoughts are underlined for emphasis. This messy vitality serves an important purpose because it shows students that the process of building knowledge is an energetic, evolving process, filled with stops and starts and detours and epiphanies (Figure C.3).

Perhaps the central purpose of making thinking visible is to provide teachers and students with physical documentation that allows them to see evidence of learning and to reflect on the learning process. For example, as students write down or draw the parts of an object they are examining, the documentation can make visible shifts in perception, such as when students suddenly discern a new kind of detail. Similarly, as students make diagrams in the Parts, People, Interactions thinking routine, their visible artifacts can reveal moments of insight regarding the complexity they are exploring, such as when they notice that people play multiple roles in a system, or that the causal relationships among parts of a system can be both linear and cyclical. The important point about visible thinking is that it plays an active role in the learning process by providing students and teachers with documentation of thinking in action that can be reflected upon, examined, probed, and changed.[10] As we and others begin down the path toward developing assessment and documentation strategies for maker-centered learning, we hope to leverage a variety of technologies—from smartphone apps to chart paper and markers—for making thinking and learning visible in the maker-centered classroom.

A final question we have about the future of maker-centered learning is how—and indeed if—it will define itself as a field. Though strands of maker-centered learning can be found in long-standing educational practices and past pedagogical theory, as a unified body of work maker-centered learning does not neatly fall into any one category. Much of this has to do with the fact that it involves the incorporation of practices from multiple disciplines, rather than being a discrete discipline itself. Perhaps, as Joi Ito likes to say about the work he engages in with his colleagues at the MIT Media Lab,[11] maker-centered learning will become an *antidiscipline*—a connected fabric of invention and innovation that brings together many disciplines but resists the siloing associated with the traditional disciplines.

Will maker-centered learning become a field or a profession? Perhaps, but as it exists now, maker-centered learning lacks the structures that make up fields and professions, among them annual conferences and peer-reviewed journals where practitioners share new ideas, a professional association that oversees the field and the profession, and degree-granting institutions where aspiring professionals can be trained and licensed for participation in the field. What might it mean for

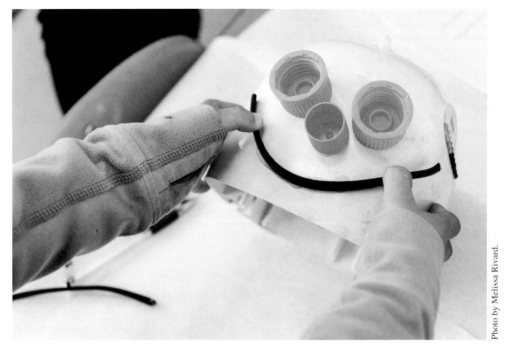

FIGURE C.3: A whimsical redesign created from the messy and evolving process of repurposing materials.

maker-centered learning to formalize itself in any of these ways? Would it stand to benefit from the formalization of its practices, or would the very essence of what makes maker-centered learning so exciting be sapped out of it through the rigors of standardization? From our current vantage point, we cannot make a prediction, but we are eager to see what happens next.

Imagine If . . .

Throughout this book one of our goals has been to introduce the wonderfully thoughtful and passionate maker educators and thought leaders we have been so lucky to meet—and to share their insights and their expertise. At the same time, it has also been our goal to provide glimpses into the array of deeply inspiring maker-centered classrooms that we have had the privilege of visiting—and to better understand what makes them tick. Whenever possible, we have also made it a priority to share the enthusiasm and passion for learning expressed by the young people that have been introduced within these pages. They include Frederica, Ana, Roberto, Cesar, and Tomas, Nala—and Jimmy.

When we think about the future of maker-centered learning, we think of these young people and their stories. Imagine if our world was full of bright, determined, empathic, and self-directed young people just like them. Young people comfortable with learning from failure like Frederica. Young people who care about their community and can navigate complex webs of social interactions to effect change in their communities like Ana. Young people who are eager to reach across social and cultural boundaries to learn from others and take charge of their own academic experiences like Roberto, Cesar, and Tomas. Young people like Nala who have developed the capacity to see the world through the lens of complex systems. And young people who will not be defeated by a broken zipper—young people who see themselves as the creators of their experiences, not just the consumers of their experiences—like Jimmy.

Now imagine an educational system that supports young learners to develop as maker-empowered citizens of the world—not just in particular neighborhoods, not just young people that share a particular set of interests—but for all young people. We cannot know what the future holds for maker-centered learning, but we can hope, we can wish, and—through thoughtful work—we can imagine if . . .

Afterword

Agency by *Design was made possible through the funding and strategic partnership of the Abundance Foundation*

In January 2012, the Abundance Foundation was entering the local philanthropic scene, aware of our inexperience, but wide-eyed in our intention to support Oakland students and educators. We knew three things: We wanted to support schools in the Temescal neighborhood of Oakland; we were deeply curious about the burgeoning maker movement in the Bay Area; and we were very excited about our early conversations with Project Zero. Beyond that, our driving purpose was to effect change for the many young people for whom education has fallen short.

What ensued was a three-year research project that led us to practice what was ultimately articulated by the Agency *by* Design initiative as a core framework—to develop the capacity to look closely, to explore complexity, and to find opportunity. Our meaningful engagement in this project—our close looking at the work from the very beginning—has made this a unique and meaningful philanthropic engagement. In the early days of Agency *by* Design, the Abundance Foundation team traveled to maker spaces with the researchers in search of what might need to be learned. We explored Project Zero ideas alongside teachers and immersed ourselves in the ideas at Project Zero's summer institute. We have had the unique experience of building this project as full partners with Project Zero, shifting the traditional grantmaker–grantee relationship and moving instead into the daily folds of work together. We looked closely at our Oakland neighborhood, Temescal, initially connecting four schools within a three-block radius, each serving different populations, and together comprising a reasonably accurate mosaic of the city. Teachers from these schools, most of whom had never done much more than walk past the

other schools in the neighborhood, had the chance to spend meaningful time in each other's classrooms.

The work of the first year evolved into a large-scale, multicity, emergent research project that provided inexhaustible opportunity to explore complexity. We engaged our first cohort of local teachers well before we settled on a research focus. Most initial members of this learning community were new to the concept of maker, and some were teaching in overcrowded, underfunded schools. The question of equity emerged as a point of discussion in the project, brought to light early on by the Oakland teachers. The maker movement itself presented rich complexities to explore: the tensions that exist between a well-resourced, white-male-dominated industry and underresourced Bay Area classrooms representing a range of communities; the relationship between expensive maker tools and the need for scaffolding around cognition within the making experience; and the (perhaps unintended) membership culture of the maker movement that leaves so many feeling left out.

Agency *by* Design has been a place for Oakland-based educators to develop their own sense of empowerment, to grow as professionals, and to find opportunity and support for creativity in resource-limited settings. With each year, our teachers blossomed as practitioners, teacher leaders, researchers, and makers. The spirit of the maker movement, coupled with their steadfast commitment to bringing equity into the conversation, made for an essential Oakland-born voice that emerged from our teachers and was heard. These teachers pushed us as a foundation and as researchers. And from that place came a deep sense of empowerment, a carving out of an Agency *by* Design Oakland identity.

The strength of the Oakland-based teacher researchers led the Abundance Foundation to establish a robust Maker Empowerment Grants program through which we support schools and organizations to embed maker-centered learning with a focus on equity. Our Agency *by* Design teacher leaders are coaching the next generation of Agency *by* Design teacher leaders in the spirit of maker empowerment, and together they are forming a network inspired and ready to disseminate the work. Their local impact is significant, and they are participating in the national conversation around making in schools. As we turn to Agency *by* Design Phase II, with a focus on assessment and documentation in the maker-centered

context, Oakland teachers are engaged as leaders and thought partners, ready to dive deep again.

So here we are, no longer inexperienced in the work, and with textured and complex stories to tell. We have been honored to work with and learn from both Project Zero and the extraordinary teachers in Oakland. And it is our intention that the findings of this work will live on to affect meaningful and sustainable change for students, educators, and schools.

Wendy Donner, *Education Program Director of the Abundance Foundation*

Appendix A: Overview of interview participants

K–12 Schools and Programs	
David Clifford	Founding Director of Innovation and Outreach, East Bay School for Boys, Berkeley, CA
Jaymes Dec	Fab Lab Coordinator, Marymount School for Girls, New York, NY
Youssou Fall	Technical Arts Teacher, Lick-Wilmerding High School, San Francisco, CA
Gus Goodwin	Technology Teacher, King Middle School, Portland, ME
Bruce Hamren	Science Faculty Teacher, The Athenian School, Danville, CA
Peter McKenna	Technology Teacher, Fox Meadow School, Scarsdale, NY
Pamela R. Moran	Superintendent, Albemarle County Public Schools, Albemarle County, VA
Gever Tulley	Founder and Education Architect, Brightworks, San Francisco, CA
Duncan Wilson	Principal, Fox Meadow School, Scarsdale, NY
Afterschool Programs	
Andy Forest	Founder, MakerKids, Toronto, ON
Mariano Ulibarri	Founder, Parachute Factory, Las Vegas, NM
School Partnerships	
Jeremy Boyle	Co-director, Children's Innovation Project, Pittsburgh, PA
Melissa Butler	Co-director, Children's Innovation Project, Pittsburgh, PA
Steve Davee	Director of Education, Maker Education Initiative, Oakland, CA
Susie Wise	Instructional Leader, K–12 Lab Nueva School/Hasso Plattner Institute of Design, Stanford University, Hillsborough/Stanford, CA

(continued)

(CONTINUED)

Museums	
Karen Wilkinson	Director of the Learning Studio, Exploratorium, San Francisco, CA
Libraries	
Steve Teeri	Founder, HYPE Teen Center, Detroit Public Library, Detroit, MI
Community Makerspaces	
Jeff Sturges	Conductor, Mt. Elliott Makerspace, Detroit, MI

Appendix B: Thinking Routines

PARTS, PURPOSES, COMPLEXITIES
LOOKING CLOSELY

Choose an object or system and ask:

What are its **parts**?
> What are its various pieces or components?

What are its **purposes**?
> What are the purposes for each of these parts?

What are its **complexities**?
> How is it complicated in its parts and purposes,
> the relationship between the two, or in other ways?

Parts, Purposes, and Complexities

What Kind of Thinking Does This Routine Encourage?
This thinking routine helps students slow down and make careful, detailed observations by encouraging them to look beyond the obvious features of an object or system. This thinking routine helps stimulate curiosity, raises questions, and surfaces areas for further inquiry.

When and How Can This Routine Be Used?
This thinking routine can be used to explore any object or system. This routine can be used on its own, or in combination with another routine. Here are some ideas and considerations for putting this thinking routine into practice:

- The routine provides an opportunity to make students' thinking visible through creating lists, maps, and drawings of the parts, purposes, complexities of various objects and systems. You may introduce the three elements of this routine all at once, or you may want to introduce the three elements of the routine one at a time.
- If an object students are working with is present and/or physically visible, students might not need a lot of background knowledge. However, if students are working with a system—like democracy—it may be helpful for students to have background knowledge or to give them an opportunity to reflect on their experiences interacting with that particular system.
- To take this routine to the next level, after students have considered the parts, purposes, and complexities of an object as it is, you may consider having students take apart the objects they are working with—and then continue to identify the parts, purposes, and complexities they notice using different colored markers.
- You may consider swapping out the word "complexities" for more accessible terms, such as *puzzles* or *questions*.

PARTS, PEOPLE, INTERACTIONS
EXPLORING COMPLEXITY

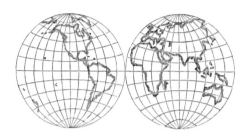

Identify a system and ask:

What are the **parts** of the system?

Who are the **people** connected to the system?

How do the people in the system **interact** with each other and with the parts of the system?

How does a change in one element of the system **affect** the various parts and people connected to the system?

Parts, People, and Interactions

What Kind of Thinking Does This Routine Encourage?
This thinking routine helps students slow down and look closely at a system. In doing so, young people are able to situate objects within systems and recognize the various people who participate—either directly or indirectly—within a particular system. Students also notice that a change in one aspect of the system may have both intended and unintended effects on another aspect of the system. When considering the parts, people, and interactions within a system, young people begin to notice the multitude of subsystems within systems. This thinking routine helps stimulate curiosity, raises questions, surfaces areas for further inquiry, and introduces *systems thinking*.

When and How Can This Routine Be Used?
This thinking routine can be used to explore any system. This routine can be used on its own, or in combination with another routine. Here are some ideas and considerations for putting this thinking routine into practice:

- Before beginning this routine, it may be helpful to lead your students towards a firm understanding of what a system is. Definitions are helpful, but we've found that concrete examples (e.g., subway systems, town recycling systems, the lunch line system at school, etc.) work best.
- In order to engage in this thinking routine, your students will have to identify a system to explore. One way to do this is to have your students situate an object within a broader system. For example, a postage stamp can be situated within the broader postal system and a bicycle helmet can be situated within a broader transportation system.
- Encourage your students to name the systems they would like to explore. This can be tricky for some students and it may be helpful for you to reorient them to an agreed upon definition of a system, or a concrete example that you shared earlier. You can then ask your students if their system meets the criteria for a system you'd discussed previously.
- Systems are made up of subsystems, and are themselves parts of broader systems. In order to avoid going down the rabbit hole of *everything is connected to everything*, it may be helpful for you to encourage your students to define the boundaries of their system.
- Working in groups, it is helpful for young people to first make a list of all of the parts, and people involved in a system, and then to map out their system on chart paper to make the interactions between all of the parts and people in their system visible.

THINK, FEEL, CARE
EXPLORING COMPLEXITY

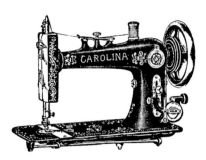

Step inside a system:

Choose a variety of people within a system and then step inside each person's point of view. As you think about what you know about the system, consider what each person might think, feel, and care about:

Think: How does this person understand this system and their role within it?

Feel: What is this person's emotional response to the system and to their position within it?

Care: What are this person's values, priorities, or motivations with regard to the system? What is important to this person?

Think, Feel, Care

What Kind of Thinking Does This Routine Encourage?
This routine encourages students to consider the different and diverse perspectives held by the various people who interact within a particular system. The goal of this routine is to help students understand that the variety of people who participate in a system think, feel, and care differently about things based on their positions in the system. This routine fosters perspective taking, raises questions, and surfaces areas for further inquiry.

When and How Can This Routine Be Used?
This thinking routine can be used to explore the perspective of any person within a particular system. This routine can be used on its own, or in combination with another routine. Here are some ideas and considerations for putting this thinking routine into practice:

- Working as individuals or in small groups, it may be helpful for you to have students sketch out a small monologue or scene that contains some of the different people who participate in a particular system. They can then assume the role of various people in their system, and act out a small scene, with each student portraying a different person's perspective.
- Once students portray a person in their system in one way, ask them how they might portray the same person in an entirely different way. This will prompt your students to understand that even within particular groups of people, there is no one perspective, but rather an array of perspectives that different and unique people may hold.
- Students should be encouraged to consider how what people think, feel, and care about may be in alignment within a particular system, or misaligned. When misalignments emerge, ask your students how these tensions are dealt with or negotiated within the system? Discussions about unequal power structures within a system may arise.
- While this routine asks students to step inside the role of a character and to imagine how they may think, feel, and what they might care about from that point of view, it is important to remember that students can never *really* know and understand someone else's perspective. When engaging in this thinking routine, it is important for students to push beyond stereotypes and to try to imagine the lived experiences of particular people. Encourage your students to develop *specific* people to play (e.g., Julia, a migrant worker, John, a used car salesman, and Martin, a Republican senator) as opposed to *types* of people (e.g., a migrant worker, a used car salesman, and a Republican senator).
- When perspective taking, students will likely draw on their assumptions about the various types of people represented in their system. As they do so, you may lead students in a discussion that addresses where these assumptions come from. You can encourage students to challenge their assumptions by asking them what they really know about someone else's perspective, and what they may need to do (e.g., conduct interviews, speak with a grandparent, etc.) in order to find out more about someone else's perspective.

IMAGINE IF…
FINDING OPPORTUNITY

Choose an object or system:

Consider the parts, purposes, and people who interact with your object or system, and then ask:

In what ways could it be made to be more **effective**?

In what ways could it be made to be more **efficient**?

In what ways could it be made to be more **ethical**?

In what ways could it be made to be more **beautiful**?

Imagine If…

What Kind of Thinking Does This Routine Encourage?
This routine first encourages divergent thinking, as students think of new possibilities for an object or system, and then encourages convergent thinking, as students decide upon an effective approach to build, tinker, re/design, or hack an object or a system. Ultimately, this thinking routine is about finding opportunity and pursuing new ideas.

When and How Can This Routine Be Used?
This thinking routine can be used to explore the possibilities of improving, tinkering with, or tweaking any object or system. Though this routine can be used on its own, we strongly suggest that it be used in combination with other Agency *by* Design thinking routines in order to best inform students of the ways in which they may improve upon a particular object or system. Here are some ideas and considerations for putting this thinking routine into practice:

- This thinking routine asks students to imagine new ways to improve an object or system by looking at the possibility space around an object or system through four different lenses. Specifically, it asks *in what ways can an object or system be made to be more effective, efficient, ethical, or beautiful?* While we find these four lenses helpful to consider, you and your students are encouraged to come up with others.
- When engaging with this thinking routine one's instinct may be to say to her students "the sky's the limit." While it is important for students to generate ideas within a wide-open possibility space, we've also found it helpful to place creative constraints on people's thinking. You may do this by limiting the variety of tools and materials students have access to, presenting certain functionality criteria, or identifying a particular population or user group. For example, in a chair re/design activity, students may be told they can only use cardboard and document fasteners, their new chair models have to be able to hold the instructor's weight, and their chairs have to be designed for people who commute to work on the subway each day.
- When considering how to redesign or hack an object or system, it is exciting to see students generate a list of wild, *blue-sky* ideas, but it is also important for students to be sensitive to the design of their objects or systems. To do this, we recommend educators have their students circle back to the other Agency *by* Design thinking routines as they search for new opportunities and brainstorm new possibilities. Likewise, if students get stuck and struggle to generate new ideas, circling back to the other AbD thinking routines may help them find opportunity and see new possibilities for their objects or systems.

Notes

Introduction

1. See White House, "#NationofMakers," retrieved from http://www.whitehouse.gov/nation-of-makers.
2. Ibid.
3. See Jennifer Oxman Ryan, "Maker Education Is About More Than 3-D Printers," *Education Week* (November 3, 2015). Retrieved from http://www.edweek.org/ew/articles/2015/11/04/maker-education-is-about-more-than-3-d.html
4. See Chris Anderson, *Makers: The New Industrial Revolution* (New York: Crown Business, 2012).
5. For more information about the Abundance Foundation, see http://www.abundance.org/
6. See Leah Buechley, "Thinking about making" (2013), retrieved from http://edstream.stanford.edu/Video/Play/883b61dd951d4d3f90abeec65eead2911d
7. Ibid.
8. See Erica Rosenfeld Halverson and Kimberly M. Sheridan, "The Maker Movement in Education," *Harvard Educational Review,* Vol. 84, No. 4, 2014, pp. 495–504, p. 502.
9. Ibid.
10. See, e.g., David Gauntlett, *Making Is Connecting: The Social Meaning of Creativity from DIY and Knitting to YouTube and Web 2.0* (Malden, MA: Polity Press, 2011); David Lang, *Zero to Maker: Learn (Just Enough) to Make (Just About) Anything* (Sebastopol, CA: Maker Media, 2013).
11. For a full discussion of a symptoms-based approach for describing complex phenomena see Nelson Goodman, *Languages of Art: An Approach to a Theory of Symbols* (Indianapolis, IN: Hackett, 1968); Nelson Goodman, *Ways of Worldmaking.* (Indianapolis, IN: Hackett, 1978).
12. See Erica Rosenfeld Halverson and Kimberly M. Sheridan, discussion of "makerspaces" as "communities of practice" (pp. 501–502) in "The Maker Movement in Education," *Harvard Educational Review,* Vol. 84, No. 4 (2014).
13. See http://sylviashow.com/ and http://cainesarcade.com/

Chapter One

1. Our use of the phrase "popular press" refers to newspaper and magazine articles, trade book publications, blogs, public radio stories, and political messaging. For a detailed discussion of our review of the popular press, see Jennifer Oxman Ryan, "Maker Education Is About More Than 3-D Printers" (2015), retrieved from http://www.edweek.org/ew/articles/2015/11/04/maker-education-is-about-more-than-3-d.html

2. See Mark Frauenfelder, "School for Hackers: The Do-It-Yourself Movement Revives Learning by Doing," *The Atlantic* (October, 2010), p. 44; Stephen Abram, "Makerspaces in Libraries, Education, and Beyond," *Internet@Schools* (March–April 2013), pp. 18–20; David V. Loertscher, "Maker Spaces and the Learning Commons," *Teacher Librarian,* Vol. 39 No. 6 (2012) pp. 45–46; Jonathan Lash, "DIY or Die: Why We Need to Teach Kids Practical Skills," *Chronicle of Higher Education*, Letters to the Editor (March 4, 2012).

3. See Chris Anderson, *Makers: The New Industrial Revolution* (New York: Crown Business, 2012).

4. Though our review of the popular press included publications that reached international audiences, the economic narrative we encountered was largely focused on the reinvigoration/reinvention of the U.S. economy.

5. See Margaret Honey, "Encouraging the Hand/Mind Connection in the Classroom," *Education Week,* retrieved from http://www.edweek.org/ew/articles/2011/02/02/19honey.h30.html para 12.

6. See Thomas Kalil, "Have Fun—Learn Something, Do Something, Make Something," in M. Honey and D. E. Kanter (Eds.), *Design, Make, Play* (New York: Routledge, 2013, pp. 12–16); OECD, "PISA 2009 Results: What Students Know and Can Do—Student Performance in Reading, Mathematics and Science," Volume I, (2010), retrieved from http://dx.doi.org/10.1787/9789264091450-en

7. See National Research Council, *A Framework for the K–12 Science Standards: Practices, Cross-cutting Concepts, and Core Ideas, Committee on Conceptual Framework for the New K–12 Science Standards, Board on Science Education, National Research Council* (Washington, DC: National Academies Press, 2012), retrieved from http://www.nap.edu/catalog/13165/a-framework-for-k-12-science-education-practices-crosscutting-concepts

8. See *President's Council of Advisers on Science and Technology Prepare and Inspire: K-12 Science, Technology, Engineering, and Math (STEM) Education for America's Future* (2010) p. 3, retrieved from https://www.whitehouse.gov/sites/default/files/microsites/ostp/pcast-stemed-report.pdf

9. For a blog post describing the coding and analysis process of this data, see Sarah May, "Exploring Complexity in Qualitative Research: Designing a System for Collaborative Analysis" (May 22, 2015), retrieved from http://www.agencybydesign.org/exploring-complexity-in-qualitative-research-designing-a-system-for-collaborative-analysis/

10. Other researchers and maker-centered learning advocates have likewise identified agency as a core outcome associated with making experiences; see, e.g., Colin Angevine and Josh Weisgrau, "Situating Makerspaces in Schools," *Digital Pedagogy Lab*, September 24, 2015, retrieved from http://www.digitalpedagogylab.com/hybridped/situating-makerspaces-in-schools/; Karen Cator, "What Kind of Smart Are You: How 'Maker' Education Is Priming Our Kids for the Kinds of Intelligence That Matters Most," *Bright* (October 14, 2015), retrieved from https://medium.com/bright/what-kind-of-smart-are-you-f6d09dfc389a#.95bxd0wpm; Lee Martin, "The Promise of the Maker Movement for Education," *Journal of Pre-College Engineering Education Research,* Vol. 5, No. 1, 2015, pp. 30–39.

11. For a related discussion of the relationship between "interest, identity, and content area knowledge," see Martin, "Promise of the Maker Movement," p. 34.

12. See Camille A. Farrington, Melissa Roderick, Elaine Allensworth, Jenny Nagaoka, Tasha Seneca Keyes, David W. Johnson, and Nicole O. Beechum, *Teaching Adolescents to Become Learners: The Role of Noncognitive Factors in Shaping School Performance: A Critical Literature Review* (Chicago, IL: The University of Chicago Consortium on Chicago School Research, 2012), p. 2.

13. Ibid, p. 4.

14. See AnnMarie Thomas, *Making Makers: Kids, Tools, and the Future of Innovation*, (Sebastopol, CA: Maker Media, 2015). For a similar study, see also Andrew Milne, Bernhard Rieckle, and Alissa Antle, "Exploring Maker Practice: Common Attitudes, Habits, and Skills from Vancouver's Maker Community," paper presented at FabLearn 2014, October 25–26, 2014, Stanford, CA.

15. See Thomas, *Making Makers* p. 5.

16. See Cator, "What Kind of Smart Are You"; Martin, "Promise of the Maker Movement"; Milne et al., "Exploring Maker Practice."

17. See Angela L. Duckworth, Christopher Peterson, Michael D. Matthews, and Dennis R. Kelly, "Grit: Perseverance and Passion for Long Term Goals," *Journal of Personality and Social Psychology*, Vol. 92, No. 6 (2007), pp. 1087–88.

18. It is important to note here that we are sensitive to the many critiques of the concept of *grit*. In particular, we recognize that "pulling yourself up by your bootstraps" does little to address the inequalities that advantage some students over others.

19. Here we find it important to note that we are sensitive to the debate over the use of the term *failure* in maker-centered learning environments. Oftentimes, the word failure has a much different meaning within the maker-centered classroom than it does throughout the rest of a school setting. The challenge to educators is to negotiate between maker-centered learning environments where failure is celebrated and the rest of young people's school-life experiences, where failure often holds dire consequences. For more on this discussion see Edward Clapp, "Reconsidering Failure in Maker-

Centered Learning" (February 2, 2015), retrieved from http://www.agencybydesign.org/reconsidering-failure-in-maker-centered-learning/

20. The name "Frederica" is used as a pseudonym.

21. See Ron Berger, *An Ethic of Excellence: Building a Culture of Craftsmanship with Students* (Portsmouth, NH: Heinemann, 2003), p. 1.

22. See http://www.designkit.org/human-centered-design (para 1); see also IDEO, *The Field Guide to Human-Centered Design* (IDEO, 2015).

Chapter Two

1. See John Dewey, *The Child and the Curriculum* (Chicago: University of Chicago Press, 1902); John Dewey, *Democracy and Education: An Introduction to the Philosophy of Education* (New York: Macmillan, 1916).

2. See Dewey, *Democracy and Education*, p. 181.

3. See Jean Piaget, *The Child's Conception of the World* (London: Routledge and Kegan Paul, 1928).

4. See Seymour Papert and Idit Harel, *Constructionism: Research Reports and Essays, 1985–1991* (Norwood, NJ: Ablex Publishing Corporation, 1991), p. 1.

5. See Lev S. Vygotsky, *Mind in Society: The Development of Higher Psychological Processes* (Cambridge, MA: Harvard University Press, 1978), p. 86.

6. See Joseph S. Krajcik and Phyllis C. Blumenfeld, "Project-Based Learning," in R. Keith Sawyer (Ed.), *The Cambridge Handbook of the Learning Sciences* (New York: Cambridge University Press, pp. 317–334), p. 318.

7. See Sylvia Libow Martinez and Gary Stager, *Invent to Learn: Making, Tinkering, and Engineering in the Classroom* (Torrance, CA: Constructing Modern Knowledge Press, 2013), p. 32.

8. Badging is the practice of acknowledging student accomplishments or specific student competencies (e.g., how to use a sewing machine, how to use a soldering iron) achieved by young people in some maker-centered classrooms.

9. The name "Terence" is used as a pseudonym.

10. See Emily R. Lai, *Collaboration: A Literature Review* (Pearson Assessments, 2011), retrieved from http://images.pearsonassessments.com/images/tmrs/Collaboration-Review.pdf

11. For more on collaborative, group, and distributed creativity see Edward P. Clapp, *Participatory Creativity: Introducing Access and Equity to the Creative Classroom* (New York: Routledge, 2016); Vlad Petre Glăveanu, *Distributed Creativity: Thinking Outside the Box of the Creative Individual* (Cham, Switzerland: Springer International Publishing, 2014); Michael Hanchett Hanson, *Worldmaking: Psychology and the Ideology of Creativity* (New York: Palgrave Macmillan, 2015); R. Keith Sawyer, *Group Creativity: Music,*

Theater, Collaboration (Mahwah, NJ: Lawrence Erlbaum Associates); R. Keith Sawyer and Stacey DeZutter, "Distributed Creativity: How Collective Creations Emerge from Collaboration," *Psychology of Aesthetics, Creativity, and the Arts,* Vol. 3, No. 2 (2009).

12. Laura Fleming nicely situates making within the context of participatory culture. See Laura Fleming, *Worlds of Making: Best Practices for Establishing a Makerspace for Your School* (Thousand Oaks, CA: Corwin, 2015). See also Henry Jenkins and colleagues, *Confronting the Challenges of Participatory Culture: Media Education for the 21st Century* (Cambridge: Massachusetts Institute of Technology Press, 2009); Kevin Slavin, "Design as Participation," *Journal of Design and Science* (February 24, 2016), retrieved from http://jods.mitpress.mit.edu/pub/design-as-participation; Edward P. Clapp, *Participatory Creativity*.

13. See David Lang, *Zero to Maker: Learn (Just Enough) to Make (Just About) Anything* (Sebastopol, CA: Maker Media, 2013).

14. This is a concept that Edith K. Ackermann also refers to as "Be In It Together," or BIIT. See Edith K. Ackermann, *Cultures of Creativity and Modes of Appropriation: From DIY to BIIT* (Billund, DK: LEGO Foundation, 2013), retrieved from http://www.legofoundation.com/en-us/research-and-learning/foundation-research/cultures-creativity

15. See http://www.p21.org/component/content/article/263-collaboration-skills

16. See Ackerman, *Cultures of Creativity,* p. 4.

17. See Ron Berger, *An Ethic of Excellence: Building a Culture of Craftsmanship with Students* (Portsmouth, NH: Heinemann, 2003), pp. 92–93.

18. See Karen Wilkinson and Mike Petrich, *The Art of Tinkering* (San Francisco, CA: Weldon Owen/Exploratorium, 2013), p. 13.

19. See Louise Boyd Cadwell, *Bringing Reggio Emilia Home: An Innovative Approach to Early Childhood Education* (New York: Teachers College Press, 1997).

20. See Rachelle Doorley, *Tinkerlab: A Hands-On Guide for Little Inventors* (Boston, MA: Roost Books, 2014); Laura Fleming, *Worlds of Making;* Scott Doorley and Scott Withhoft, *Make Space: How to Set the Stage for Creative Collaboration* (New York: John Wiley & Sons, 2012).

21. See Mark Hatch, *The Maker Manifesto: Rules for Innovation in the New World of Crafters, Hackers, and Tinkerers* (New York: McGraw-Hill Education, 2014).

22. Ibid, pp. 24–26.

Chapter Three

1. See Albert Bandura, "Towards a Psychology of Human Agency," *Perspectives on Psychological Science,* Vol. 1, No. 164 (2006), p. 164.

2. Ibid.

3. Ibid., p. 165.

4. The name "Ana" is used as a pseudonym.

5. See Bandura, "Towards a Psychology of Human Agency" (2006), p. 164.

6. See Albert Bandura, "Exercise of Human Agency Through Collective Efficacy," *Current Directions in Psychological Science* Vol. 9, No. 3 (2000), p. 75.

7. See Brittany Harker Martin, "Social Empowerment: The Evolution of a Model to Measure the Effects of Arts Integration and Other Forms of Socially Empowered Learning" (under review).

8. See David Lang, *Zero to Maker: Learn (Just Enough) to Make (Just About) Anything* (Sebastopol, CA: Maker Media, 2013), p. 19.

9. See Fleming, *Worlds of Making: Best Practices for Establishing a Makerspace for Your School* (Thousand Oaks, CA: Corwin, 2015); Henry Jenkins and colleagues, *Confronting the Challenges of Participatory Culture: Media Education for the 21st Century* (Cambridge: Massachusetts Institute of Technology Press, 2009); Kevin Slavin, "Design as Participation," *Journal of Design and Science* (February 24, 2016), retrieved from http://jods.mitpress.mit.edu/pub/design-as-participation; Edward Clapp, *Participatory Creativity: Introducing Access and Equity to the Creative Classroom* (New York: Routledge, 2016) and Michael Hanchett Hanson, *Worldmaking: Psychology and the Ideology of Creativity* (New York: Palgrave Macmillan, 2015).

10. "Roberto," "Cesar," and "Tomas" are used as pseudonyms.

11. See IDEO's *Field Guide to Human-Centered Design* (2015), p. 20, retrieved from http://www.designkit.org/resources/1

12. See Thomas J. Peters and Robert H. Waterman, *In Search of Excellence: Lessons from America's Best Run Companies* (New York: HarperCollins, 1982).

13. For more information regarding the Abundance Foundation's empowerment initiatives see http://www.abundance.org/empowerment/

14. Ibid, para 1.

15. See Lauren M. Stevenson, *Setting the Agenda: National Summit on Creative Youth Development* (Boston, MA: Massachusetts Cultural Council, 2014), p. 1, retrieved from http://www.massculturalcouncil.org/Setting_the_Agenda.pdf

16. See David N. Perkins, Shari Tishman, Ron Ritchhart, Kiki Donis, and Al Andrade, "Intelligence in the Wild: A Dispositional View of Intellectual Traits," *Educational Psychology Review*, Vol. 12, No. 3 (2000), 269–293; Ron Ritchhart, *Intellectual Character: What It Is, Why It Matters, and How to Get It* (San Francisco, CA: Jossey-Bass, 2002); Shari Tishman, "Added Value: A Dispositional Perspective on Thinking," in Arthur L. Costa (Ed.), *Developing Minds: A Resource Book for Teaching Thinking* (3rd ed., Alexandria, VA: Association for Supervision and Curriculum Development, 2001).

17. See Perkins et al., "Intelligence in the Wild" (2000).

Chapter Four

1. See Kyle Wiens, "The New MacBook Pro: Unfixable, Unhackable, Untenable," *Wired* (June 14, 2012), retrieved from http://www.wired.com/2012/06/opinion-apple-retina-displa/, para 2.

2. See Jennifer Oxman Ryan, "The Maker Mind," TEDx Dirigo Generate, Brunswick, ME, November 2013, retrieved from https://www.youtube.com/watch?v=cI2cMyOZVgE

3. See Kyle Wiens, "The Repair Revolution," in Todd McLellan, *Things Come Apart: A Tear Down Manual for Modern Living* (London: Thames & Hudson, 2013), pp. 40–43, p. 41.

4. Ibid, p. 43.

5. For a fun example of an attempt at taking apart a doorknob and making the tough decision to call a locksmith or do-it-yourself, see Tatum Omari's blog post "Agency (and Comedy) by Design" on the Agency *by* Design website http://www.agencybydesign.org/agency-and-comedy-by-design-2/

6. See Wiens, "Repair Revolution," p. 43.

7. See David Perkins, *Knowledge as Design* (Hillsdale, NJ: L. Erlbaum Associates, 1986), p. 2.

8. Ibid, p. 2.

9. See Robert E. Haskell, *Transfer of Learning: Cognition, Instruction, and Reasoning* (Orlando, FL: Harcourt, 2001); Gavriel Salomon and David N. Perkins, "Rocky Roads to Transfer: Rethinking Mechanisms of a Neglected Phenomenon," *Educational Psychologist*, Vol. 24, No. 2 (1989), 113–142; D. L. Schwartz, S. Varma, and L. Martin, "Dynamic Transfer and Innovation," in S. Vosniadou (Ed.), *International Handbook of Research on Conceptual Change* (New York: Routledge, 2008), pp. 479–506.

10. Here, "Nala" is used as a pseudonym.

11. See Linda Booth Sweeney, "Learning to Connect the Dots: Developing Children's Systems Literacy," *Solutions*, Vol. 5, No. 3 (2012), pp. 55–62.

12. For the full text of Tatum's blog post, see http://www.agencybydesign.org/agency-and-comedy-by-design-2/

13. See Ernesto Oroza, "Technological Disobedience," *Makeshift: A Journal of Hidden Creativity*, Vol. 1, No. 3 (2012), pp. 50–53, retrieved from http://mkshft.org/technological-disobedience/ see also http://www.vice.com/video/the-technological-disobedience-of-ernesto-oroza

14. See Oroza, "Technological Disobedience," p. 50.

15. Ibid, pp. 50–52.

16. Ibid, pp. 52–53.

17. Ibid, p. 50.

Chapter Five

1. See Shari Tishman, "Slow Looking and Complexity," *Out of Eden Learn Blog*, July 21, 2014, retrieved from https://walktolearn.outofedenwalk.com/2014/07/21/slow-looking-and-complexity/

2. See https://www.youtube.com/watch?v=zZHp1fGdAWE

3. See Maxine Greene, "Thinking of Things as If They Could be Otherwise: The Arts and Intimations of a Better Social Order," in *Variations on a Blue Guitar: The Lincoln Center Institute Lectures on Aesthetic Education* (New York: Teachers College Press, 2001/1997, pp. 116–121).

4. For more about the Visible Thinking, Artful Thinking, and Cultures of Thinking projects, please visit the Project Zero website: http://www.pz.harvard.edu/

5. See David Perkins, *Knowledge as Design* (Hillsdale, NJ: L. Erlbaum Associates, 1986).

6. For more on the Artful Thinking project, see http://pzartfulthinking.org/.

7. See Shari Tishman, "The Object of Their Attention," *Educational Leadership*, Vol. 65, No. 5 (2008), pp. 44–46, p. 45.

8. See IDEO, *The Field Guide to Human-Centered Design* (2015), retrieved from http://www.designkit.org/resources/1

9. See Kevin Slavin "Design as Participation," *Journal of Design and Science*, 2016 retrieved from http://jods.mitpress.mit.edu/pub/design-as-participation, para 15.

10. Ibid, para 22.

11. Ibid, paras 40–41.

Conclusion

1. See https://defdist.org/about/.

2. See Tim Maly, "Thingiverse Removes (Most) Printable Gun Parts," *Wired*, December 19, 2012, retrieved from http://www.wired.com/2012/12/thingiverse-removes-gun-parts/

3. For an interesting discussion concerning the ethical dimensions of making see John Tierney, "The Dilemmas of Maker Culture," *Atlantic*, April 20, 2015, retrieved from http://www.theatlantic.com/technology/archive/2015/04/the-dilemmas-of-maker-culture/390891/

4. For critiques of the inherent biases of the maker movement, see Lisa Brahams and Kevin Crowley, "Making Sense of Making: Defining Learning Practices in *MAKE* Magazine," in K. Peppler, E. Halverson, and Y. Kafai (Eds.), *Makeology: Makers as Learners* (New York: Routledge, 2016), pp. 13–28; Leah Buechley, "Thinking About Making," keynote address, FabLearn Conference 2013, Stanford University, retrieved from http://edstream.stanford.edu/Video/Play/883b61dd951d4d3f90abeec65eead2911d;

Yasmin Kafai, Deborah A. Fields, and Kristin A. Searle, "Electronic Textiles as Disruptive Designs: Supporting and Challenging Maker Activities in Schools," *Harvard Educational Review*, Vol. 84, No. 4 (2014), pp. 532–556; Kristin A. Searle, Deborah A. Fields, and Yasmin Kafai, "Is Sewing a Girl's Sport? Addressing Gender Issues in the Maker Culture," in K. Peppler, E. Halverson, and Y. Kafai (Eds.), *Makeology: Makers as Learners* (New York: Routledge, 2016), pp. 72–84; Shirin Vossoughi, Paula K. Hooper, and Meg Escudé, "Making Through the Lens of Culture and Power: Toward Transformative Visions of Educational Equity," *Harvard Educational Review*, Vol. 86, No. 2, 2016, pp. 206–232; Debbie Chachra, "Why I Am Not a Maker," The Atlantic (2015), retrieved from http://www.theatlantic.com/technology/archive/2015/01/why-i-am-not-a-maker/384767/.

5. See Mindy L. Kornhaber, Kelly Griffith, and Alison Tyler, "It's Not Education by Zipcode Anymore—But What Is It? Conceptions of Equity Under the Common Core," *Education Policy Analysis Archives*, Vol. 22, No. 4 (2014), retrieved from http://dx.doi.org/10.14507/epaa.v22n4.2014.

6. See Shirin Vossoughi, Meg Escudé, Fan Kong, and Paula Hooper, "Tinkering, Learning & Equity in the Afterschool Setting," paper presented at the FabLearn conference October 27–28, 2013, Stanford University, Stanford, CA.

7. We do, however, want to mention the efforts of the many organizations who have endeavored to build networks to support maker-centered learning, especially FabLearn, the Maker Education Initiative, the Remake Learning Network, and the many maker educator meet-ups that take place throughout the United States.

8. For more about Project Zero research on making thinking and learning visible, please visit the Making Learning Visible (http://www.pz.harvard.edu/projects/making-learning-visible) and Visible Thinking (http://www.pz.harvard.edu/projects/visible-thinking) project pages on the Project Zero website.

9. See Shari Tishman and Patricia Palmer, "Visible Thinking," *Leadership Compass,* Vol. 2, No. 4 (2005), pp. 1–3, p. 1.

10. See Mara Krechevsky, Ben Mardell, Melissa Rivard, and Daniel Wilson, *Visible Learners: Promoting Reggio-Inspired Approaches in All Schools* (San Francisco, CA: Jossey-Bass, 2013).

11. See Joi Ito, "Antidisciplinary," retrieved from http://joi.ito.com/weblog/2014/10/02/antidisciplinar.html.

References

Clapp, E. P. (2016). *Participatory creativity: Introducing access and equity in the creative classroom*. New York: Routledge.

Committee on Conceptual Framework for the New K–12 Science Standards/National Research Council. (2012). *Framework for K–12 science education: Practices, cross-cutting concepts, and core ideas*. Washington, D.C.: National Academies Press. Retrieved from: http://www.nap.edu/catalog.php?record_id=13165

Dewey, J. (1902). *The child and the curriculum*. Chicago: University of Chicago Press.

Dewey, J. (1916). *Democracy and education: An introduction to the philosophy of education*. New York: Macmillan.

Dewey, J. (1980/1934). *Art as experience*. New York: Perigee Books.

Doorley, R. (2014). *Tinkerlab: A hands-on guide for little inventors*. Boston, MA: Roost Books.

Doorley S., & Withhoft, S. (2012). *Make space: How to set the stage for creative collaboration*. New York: John Wiley & Sons.

Dougherty, D. (2012). The maker movement. *Innovations: Technology, Governance, Globalization, 7*(3), 11–14.

Dougherty, D. (2013). The maker mindset. In M. Honey & D. E. Kanter (Eds.), *Design, make, play: Growing the next generation of STEM innovators* (pp. 7–11). New York: Routledge.

Duckworth, A. L., Peterson, C., Mathews, M. D., & Kelly, D. R. (2007). Grit: Perseverance and passion for long term goals. *Journal of Personality and Social Psychology, 92*(6), 1087–1101.

Economist (2011, December 3). More than just digital quilting.

Farrington, C. A., Roderick, M., Allensworth, E., Nagaoka, J., Keyes, T. S., Johnson, D. W., & Beechum, N. O. (2012). *Teaching adolescents to become learners: The role of noncognitive factors in shaping school performance: A critical literature review*. Chicago, IL: University of Chicago Consortium on Chicago School Research.

Fleming, L. (2015). *Worlds of making: Best practices for establishing a makerspace for your school*. Thousand Oaks, CA: Corwin.

Frauenfelder, M. (2010, October). School for hackers: The do-it-yourself movement revives learning by doing. *The Atlantic*, p. 44.

Gauntlett, D. (2011). *Making is connecting: The social meaning of creativity from DIY and knitting to YouTube and Web 2.0*. Malden, MA: Polity Press.

Glăveanu, V. P. (2014). *Distributed creativity: Thinking outside the box of the creative individual*. Cham, Switzerland: Springer International Publishing.

Goodman, N. (1968). *Languages of art: An approach to a theory of symbols*. Indianapolis, IN: Hackett.

Goodman, N. (1978). *Ways of worldmaking*. Indianapolis, IN: Hackett.

Greene, M. (2001/1997). Thinking of things as if they could be otherwise: The arts and intimations of a better social order, in *Variations on a blue guitar: The Lincoln Center Institute lectures on aesthetic education* (pp. 116–121). New York: Teachers College Press.

References

Clapp, E. P. (2016). *Participatory creativity: Introducing access and equity in the creative class-room*. New York: Routledge.

Committee on Conceptual Framework for the New K–12 Science Standards/National Research Council. (2012). *Framework for K–12 science education: Practices, cross-cutting concepts, and core ideas*. Washington, D.C.: National Academies Press. Retrieved from: http://www.nap.edu/catalog.php?record_id=13165

Dewey, J. (1902). *The child and the curriculum*. Chicago: University of Chicago Press.

Dewey, J. (1916). *Democracy and education: An introduction to the philosophy of education*. New York: Macmillan.

Dewey, J. (1980/1934). *Art as experience*. New York: Perigee Books.

Doorley, R. (2014). *Tinkerlab: A hands-on guide for little inventors*. Boston, MA: Roost Books.

Doorley S., & Withhoft, S. (2012). *Make space: How to set the stage for creative collaboration*. New York: John Wiley & Sons.

Dougherty, D. (2012). The maker movement. *Innovations: Technology, Governance, Globalization, 7*(3), 11–14.

Dougherty, D. (2013). The maker mindset. In M. Honey & D. E. Kanter (Eds.), *Design, make, play: Growing the next generation of STEM innovators* (pp. 7–11). New York: Routledge.

Duckworth, A. L., Peterson, C., Mathews, M. D., & Kelly, D. R. (2007). Grit: Perseverance and passion for long term goals. *Journal of Personality and Social Psychology, 92*(6), 1087–1101.

Economist (2011, December 3). More than just digital quilting.

Farrington, C. A., Roderick, M., Allensworth, E., Nagaoka, J., Keyes, T. S., Johnson, D. W., & Beechum, N. O. (2012). *Teaching adolescents to become learners: The role of noncognitive factors in shaping school performance: A critical literature review*. Chicago, IL: University of Chicago Consortium on Chicago School Research.

Fleming, L. (2015). *Worlds of making: Best practices for establishing a makerspace for your school*. Thousand Oaks, CA: Corwin.

Frauenfelder, M. (2010, October). School for hackers: The do-it-yourself movement revives learning by doing. *The Atlantic,* p. 44.

Gauntlett, D. (2011). *Making is connecting: The social meaning of creativity from DIY and knitting to YouTube and Web 2.0*. Malden, MA: Polity Press.

Glăveanu, V. P. (2014). *Distributed creativity: Thinking outside the box of the creative individual*. Cham, Switzerland: Springer International Publishing.

Goodman, N. (1968). *Languages of art: An approach to a theory of symbols*. Indianapolis, IN: Hackett.

Goodman, N. (1978). *Ways of worldmaking*. Indianapolis, IN: Hackett.

Greene, M. (2001/1997). Thinking of things as if they could be otherwise: The arts and intimations of a better social order, in *Variations on a blue guitar: The Lincoln Center Institute lectures on aesthetic education* (pp. 116–121). New York: Teachers College Press.

References

Abram, S. (2013, March/April). Makerspaces in libraries, education, and beyond, *Internet@ Schools*, pp. 18–20.

Ackermann, E. K. (2013). Cultures of creativity and modes of appropriation: From DIY to BIIT. Billund, DK: LEGO Foundation. Retrieved from http://www.legofoundation.com/en-us/research-and-learning/foundation-research/cultures-creativity

Anderson, C. (2012). *Makers: The new industrial revolution*. New York: Crown Business.

Angevine, C., & Weisgrau, J. (2015, September 24). Situating makerspaces in schools. *Digital Pedagogy Lab*. Retrieved from http://www.digitalpedagogylab.com/hybridped/situating-makerspaces-in-schools/

Bandura, A. (2000). Exercise of human agency through collective efficacy. *Current Directions in Psychological Science, 9*(3), 75–78.

Bandura, A. (2006). Towards a psychology of human agency. *Perspectives on Psychological Science, 1*(2), 164–180.

Berger, R. (2003). *An ethic of excellence: Building a culture of craftsmanship with students.* Portsmouth, NH: Heinemann.

Borghans, L., Duckworth, A. L., Heckman, J. J., & ter Weel, B. (2008). The economics and psychology of personality traits. *Journal of Human Resources, 43*(4), 972–1059.

Brahams, L., & Crowley, K. (2016). Making sense of making: Defining learning practices in *MAKE* Magazine, in K. Peppler, E. Halverson, & Y. Kafai (Eds.), *Makeology: Makers as Learners* (pp. 13–28). New York: Routledge.

Buechley, L. (2013). Thinking about making. Keynote address, FabLearn Conference, Stanford University. Retrieved from http://edstream.stanford.edu/Video/Play/883b61dd951d4d3f90abeec65eead2911d

Cadwell, L. B. (1997). *Bringing Reggio Emilia home: An innovative approach to early childhood education.* New York: Teachers College Press.

Cator, K. (2015, October 14). What kind of smart are you: How "maker" education is priming our kids for the kinds of intelligence that matters most. *Bright.* Retrieved from https://medium.com/bright/what-kind-of-smart-are-you-f6d09dfc389a#.95bxd0wpm

Chachra, D. (2015). Why I am not a maker. *The Atlantic*, retrieved from http://www.theatlantic.com/technology/archive/2015/01/why-i-am-not-a-maker/384767/

Clapp, E. P. (2015, February 2). Reconsidering failure in maker-centered learning. Retrieved from http://www.agencybydesign.org/reconsidering-failure-in-maker-centered-learning/

Yasmin Kafai, Deborah A. Fields, and Kristin A. Searle, "Electronic Textiles as Disruptive Designs: Supporting and Challenging Maker Activities in Schools," *Harvard Educational Review*, Vol. 84, No. 4 (2014), pp. 532–556; Kristin A. Searle, Deborah A. Fields, and Yasmin Kafai, "Is Sewing a Girl's Sport? Addressing Gender Issues in the Maker Culture," in K. Peppler, E. Halverson, and Y. Kafai (Eds.), *Makeology: Makers as Learners* (New York: Routledge, 2016), pp. 72–84; Shirin Vossoughi, Paula K. Hooper, and Meg Escudé, "Making Through the Lens of Culture and Power: Toward Transformative Visions of Educational Equity," *Harvard Educational Review*, Vol. 86, No. 2, 2016, pp. 206–232; Debbie Chachra, "Why I Am Not a Maker," The Atlantic (2015), retrieved from http://www.theatlantic.com/technology/archive/2015/01/why-i-am-not-a-maker/384767/.

5. See Mindy L. Kornhaber, Kelly Griffith, and Alison Tyler, "It's Not Education by Zipcode Anymore—But What Is It? Conceptions of Equity Under the Common Core," *Education Policy Analysis Archives*, Vol. 22, No. 4 (2014), retrieved from http://dx.doi.org/10.14507/epaa.v22n4.2014.

6. See Shirin Vossoughi, Meg Escudé, Fan Kong, and Paula Hooper, "Tinkering, Learning & Equity in the Afterschool Setting," paper presented at the FabLearn conference October 27–28, 2013, Stanford University, Stanford, CA.

7. We do, however, want to mention the efforts of the many organizations who have endeavored to build networks to support maker-centered learning, especially FabLearn, the Maker Education Initiative, the Remake Learning Network, and the many maker educator meet-ups that take place throughout the United States.

8. For more about Project Zero research on making thinking and learning visible, please visit the Making Learning Visible (http://www.pz.harvard.edu/projects/making-learning-visible) and Visible Thinking (http://www.pz.harvard.edu/projects/visible-thinking) project pages on the Project Zero website.

9. See Shari Tishman and Patricia Palmer, "Visible Thinking," *Leadership Compass,* Vol. 2, No. 4 (2005), pp. 1–3, p. 1.

10. See Mara Krechevsky, Ben Mardell, Melissa Rivard, and Daniel Wilson, *Visible Learners: Promoting Reggio-Inspired Approaches in All Schools* (San Francisco, CA: Jossey-Bass, 2013).

11. See Joi Ito, "Antidisciplinary," retrieved from http://joi.ito.com/weblog/2014/10/02/antidisciplinar.html.

Hanchett Hanson, M. (2015). *Worldmaking: Psychology and the ideology of creativity.* New York: Palgrave Macmillan.

Haskell, R. E. (2000). *Transfer of learning: Cognition, instruction, and reasoning.* Orlando, FL: Harcourt.

Hatch, M. (2014). *The maker manifesto: Rules for innovation in the new world of crafters, hackers, and tinkerers.* New York: McGraw-Hill Education.

Honey, M. (2011). Encouraging the hand/mind connection in the classroom, *Education Week.* Retrieved from http://www.edweek.org/ew/articles/2011/02/02/19honey.h30.html

Honey, M., & Kanter, D. E. (2013). *Design, make, play: Growing the next generation of STEM innovators.* New York: Routledge.

IDEO. (2015). *The field guide to human-centered design.* Retrieved from http://www.designkit.org/resources/1

Jenkins, H., Purushotma, R., Weigel, M., Clinton, K., & Robison, A. J. (2009). *Confronting the challenges of participatory culture: Media education for the 21st century.* Cambridge: Massachusetts Institute of Technology Press.

Kafai, Y. M., Fields, D. A., & Searle, K. A. (2014). Electronic textiles as disruptive designs: Supporting and challenging maker activities in schools. *Harvard Educational Review, 84*(4), 532–556.

Kalil, T. (2013). Have fun—learn something, do something, make something. In M. Honey & D. E. Kanter (Eds.), *Design, make, play: Growing the next generation of STEM innovators* (pp. 12–16). New York: Routledge.

Kornhaber, M. L., Griffith, K., & Tyler, A. (2014). It's not education by zipcode anymore—but what is it? Conceptions of equity under Common Core. *Education Policy Analysis Archives, 22*(4). Retrieved from http://dx.doi.org/10.14507/epaa.v22n4.2014

Krajcik, J. S., & Blumenfeld, P. C. (2006). Project-based learning, in R. Keith Sawyer (Ed.), *The Cambridge Handbook of the Learning Sciences* (pp. 317–334). New York: Cambridge University Press.

Krechevesky, M. & Mardell, B. (2001). Four features of learning in groups. In Project Zero and Reggio Children, *Making learning visible: Children as individual and group learners* (pp. 284–295). Reggio Emilia, Italy: Reggio Children.

Krechevsky, M., Mardell, B., Rivard, M., & Wilson, D. (2013). *Visible learners: Promoting Reggio-inspired approaches in all schools.* San Francisco, CA: Jossey-Bass.

Lai, E. R. (2011). Collaboration: A literature review. Pearson Assessments. Retrieved from http://images.pearsonassessments.com/images/tmrs/Collaboration-Review.pdf

Lang, D. (2013). *Zero to maker: Learn (just enough) to make (just about) anything.* Sebastopol, CA: Maker Media.

Lash, J. (2012, March 4). DIY or die: Why we need to teach kids practical skills, *The Chronicle of Higher Education*, Letters to the Editor.

Loertscher, D. V. (2012). Maker spaces and the learning commons, *Teacher Librarian, 39*(6), 45–46.

Maly, T. (2012, December 19). Thingiverse removes (most) printable gun parts. *Wired.* Retrieved from http://www.wired.com/2012/12/thingiverse-removes-gun-parts/

Martin, B. H. (under review). Social empowerment: The evolution of a model to measure the effects of arts integration and other forms of socially empowered learning.

Martin, L. (2015). The promise of the maker movement for education. *Journal of Pre-College Engineering Education Research, 5*(1) 30–39.

Martinez, S. L., & Stager, G. (2013). *Invent to learn: Making, tinkering, and engineering in the classroom.* Torrance, CA: Constructing Modern Knowledge Press.

May, S. (2015, May 22). Exploring complexity in qualitative research: Designing a system for collaborative analysis. Retrieved from http://www.agencybydesign.org/exploring-complexity-in-qualitative-research-designing-a-system-for-collaborative-analysis/

McLellan, T. (2013). *Things come apart: A tear down manual for modern living.* London: Thames & Hudson.

Milne, A., Rieckle, B., & Antle, A. (2014). Exploring maker practice: Common attitudes, habits, and skills from Vancouver's maker community. Paper presented at FabLearn 2014, October 25–26, 2014, Stanford, CA.

National Research Council. (2012). A framework for the K–12 science standards: Practices, crosscutting concepts, and core ideas, Committee on Conceptual Framework for the New K–12 Science Standards, Board on Science Education, National Research Council, Washington, DC: The National Academies Press. Retrieved from http://www.nap.edu/catalog/13165/a-framework-for-k-12-science-education-practices-crosscutting-concepts

Obama, B. (2009, April 27). Remarks by the president at the national academy of sciences annual meeting. Retrieved from http://www.whitehouse.gov/the-press-office/remarks-president-national-academy-sciences-annual-meeting

Obama, B. (2009, November 23). Remarks by the president on the "Education to Innovate" campaign. Retrieved from www.whitehouse.gov/the-press-office/remarks-president-education-innovate-campaign

OECD (2010), PISA 2009 Results: What Students Know and Can Do – Student Performance in Reading, Mathematics and Science (Volume I). Retrieved from http://dx.doi.org/10.1787/9789264091450-en

Oroza, E. (2012). Technological disobedience. *Makeshift: A Journal of Hidden Creativity, 1*(3), 50–53. Retrieved from http://mkshft.org/technological-disobedience/

Papert, S., & Harel, I. (1991). *Constructionism: Research reports and essays, 1985–1991.* Ablex Publishing Corporation.

Perkins, D. (1986). *Knowledge as design.* Hillsdale, NJ: L. Erlbaum Associates.

Perkins, D. N. & Salomon, G. (1992). *Transfer of learning. International Encyclopedia of Education* (2nd ed.). Oxford, UK: Pergamon Press.

Perkins, D. N., Jay, E., & Tishman, S. (1993). Beyond abilities: A dispositional theory of thinking. *Merrill-Palmer Quarterly, 39*(1), 1–21.

Perkins, D. N., & Tishman, S. (2006). Learning that matters: Towards a dispositional perspective on education and its research needs. A report prepared for the Spencer Foundation.

Perkins, D. N., Tishman, S., Ritchhart, R., Donis, K., & Andrade, A. (2000). Intelligence in the wild: A dispositional view of intellectual traits. *Educational Psychology Review, 12*(3), 269–293.

Peters, T. J., & Waterman, R. H. (1982). *In search of excellence: Lessons from America's best run companies.* New York: HarperCollins.

President's Council of Advisers on Science and Technology (2010). Prepare and inspire: K-12 science, technology, engineering, and math (STEM) education for America's future. Retrieved from https://www.whitehouse.gov/sites/default/files/microsites/ostp/pcast-stemed-report.pdf

Ritchhart, R. (2002). *Intellectual character: What it is, why it matters, and how to get it.* San Francisco: Jossey-Bass.

Ritchhart, R., Palmer, P., Church, M., & Tishman, S. (2006). Thinking routines: Establishing patterns of thinking in the classroom. Paper presented at the American Educational Research Conference, April 7–11, San Francisco, CA. Retrieved from http://www.ronritchhart.com/Papers_files/AERA06ThinkingRoutinesV3.pdf

Royte, E. (2013, May) What lies ahead for 3D printing? The new technology promises a factory in every home—and a whole lot more. *Smithsonian.*

Ryan, J. O. (2013, November). The maker mind. TEDx Dirigo Generate, Brunswick, ME. Retrieved from https://www.youtube.com/watch?v=cI2cMyOZVgE

Ryan, J. O. (2015, November 3). Maker education is about more than 3-D printers. *Education Week.* Retrieved from http://www.edweek.org/ew/articles/2015/11/04/maker-education-is-about-more-than-3-d.html

Salomon, G., & Perkins, D. N. (1989). Rocky roads to transfer: rethinking mechanisms of a neglected phenomenon. *Educational Psychologist, 24,* 113–142.

Sawyer, R. K. (2003). *Group creativity: Music, theater, collaboration.* Mahwah, NJ: Lawrence Erlbaum Associates.

Sawyer, R. K., & DeZutter, S. (2009). Distributed creativity: How collective creations emerge from collaboration. *Psychology of Aesthetics, Creativity, and the Arts, 3*(2), 81–92.

Schwartz, D. L., Varma, S., & Martin, L. (2008). Dynamic transfer and innovation. In S. Vosniadou (Ed.), *International handbook of research on conceptual change* (pp. 479–506). New York: Routledge.

Searle, K. A., Fields, D. A., & Kafai, Y. B. (2016). Is sewing a girl's sport? Addressing gender issues in the maker culture, in K. Peppler, E. Halverson, & Y. Kafai (Eds.), *Makeology: Makers as Learners* (pp. 72–84). New York: Routledge.

Sennett, R. (2008). *The craftsman.* New Haven, CT: Yale University Press.

Sheridan, K. M., Halverson, E. R., Litts, B. K., Brahms, L., Jacobs-Priebe, L., & Owens, T. (2014). Learning in the making: A comparative case study of three makerspaces. *Harvard Educational Review, 84*(4), 505–531.

Slavin, K. (2014, February 24). Design as participation, *Journal of Design and Science.* Retrieved from http://jods.mitpress.mit.edu/pub/design-as-participation

Stevenson (2014). *Setting the agenda: National summit on creative youth development.* Boston, MA: Massachusetts Cultural Council. Retrieved from http://www.massculturalcouncil. org/Setting_the_Agenda.pdf

Sweeney, L. B. (2012). Learning to connect the dots: Developing children's systems literacy. *Solutions, 5*(3), 55–62.

Thomas, A. (2014). *Making makers: Kids, tools, and the future of innovation,* Sebastopol, CA: Maker Media.

Tierney, J. (2015, April 20). The dilemmas of maker culture. *Atlantic.* Retrieved from http://www.theatlantic.com/technology/archive/2015/04/the-dilemmas-of-maker-culture/390891/

Tishman, S. (2001). Added value: A dispositional perspective on thinking. In A. L. Costa (Ed.), *Developing minds: A resource book for teaching thinking, third edition* (pp. 72–75). Alexandria, VA: Association for Supervision and Curriculum Development.

Tishman, S. (2008). The object of their attention. *Educational Leadership, 65*(5), 44–46.

Tishman, S. (2014, July 21). Slow looking and complexity. Out of Eden Learn Blog. Retrieved from https://walktolearn.outofedenwalk.com/2014/07/21/slow-looking-and-complexity/

Tishman, S., Jay, E., & Perkins, D. N. (1993). Teaching thinking dispositions: From transmission to enculturation. *Theory into Practice, 32*(3), 147–153.

Tishman, S., & Palmer, P. (2005). Visible thinking. *Leadership Compass, 2*(4) 1–3.

Vossoughi, S., Escudé, M., Kong, F., & Hooper, P. (2013). Tinkering, learning & equity in the afterschool setting. Paper presented at the FabLearn conference, October 27–28, Stanford University, Stanford, CA.

Vossoughi, S., Hooper, P. K., & Escudé, M. (2016). Making through the lens of culture and power: Toward transformative visions of educational equity. *Harvard Educational Review, 86*(2), 206–232.

Vygotsky, L. S. (1978). *Mind in society: The development of higher psychological processes.* Cambridge, MA: Harvard University Press.

Walker, R. (2012, February). Meet your maker. *Fast Company,* 90–96.

White House. (2013, February 12). Remarks by the President in the State of the Union Address. Retrieved from https://www.whitehouse.gov/the-press-office/2013/02/12/remarks-president-state-union-address.

White House. (2014). A nation of makers. Retrieved from http://www.whitehouse.gov/nation-of-makers.

White House. (2014, June 17) Presidential Proclamation—National Day of Making, 2014. Retrieved from https://www.whitehouse.gov/the-press-office/2014/06/17/presidential-proclamation-national-day-making-2014.

Wiens, K. (2012, June 4). The new MacBook Pro: Unfixable, unhackable, untenable. *Wired.* Retrieved from http://www.wired.com/2012/06/opinion-apple-retina-displa/.

Wiens, K. (2013). The repair revolution, in T. McLellan, *Things come apart: A tear down manual for modern living* (pp. 40–43). London: Thames & Hudson, 2013.

Wilkinson, K., & Petrich, M. (2013). *The art of tinkering.* San Francisco, CA: Weldon Owen/Exploratorium.

Index

Pages followed by *fig* indicate an illustrated figure or photograph.

About the Authors

Edward P. Clapp, Ed.D.

Edward P. Clapp is a research associate at Project Zero where he is a member of the core team working on the Agency *by* Design initiative. He is also a core member of the Creating Communities of Innovation initiative, which is an action research study geared toward developing educational innovations among a network of schools in the United Arab Emirates. Edward's current research interests include creativity and innovation, maker-centered learning, design thinking, and contemporary approaches to arts teaching and learning. In addition to his work as an educational researcher, Edward is also a lecturer on education at the Harvard Graduate School of Education and co-instructor (with Jennifer Oxman Ryan) of the online course Thinking and Learning in the Maker-Centered Classroom. His most recent book, *Participatory Creativity: Introducing Access and Equity to the Creative Classroom,* was published in 2016 by Routledge.

Jessica Ross

Jessica Ross is a researcher and project manager for the Agency *by* Design research project. Previously, Jessica taught Grades 5–8 humanities for 10 years, where she integrated Project Zero frameworks including Artful Thinking and Teaching for Understanding into her classroom practice. She has a background in education, history, and writing. Jessica has collaborated with schools, school districts, and museums to integrate frameworks like Artful and Visible Thinking, along with interdisciplinary-focused curriculum design, into their programs. She is currently an education coordinator of the Project Zero Classroom Institute and a teaching fellow at the Harvard Graduate School of Education.

Jennifer O. Ryan

Jennifer O. Ryan is a researcher and project manager for the Pedagogy of Play initiative—a collaboration between Project Zero, the International School of Billund (Denmark), and LEGO Foundation that is exploring how play can assume a central role in schools. She is former project manager for Agency *by* Design and previously worked on several other projects, including Qualities of Quality: Excellence in Arts Education and How to Achieve It; and the Good Play project, focusing on the ethical dimension of young people's online activities. Jennifer's research interests include arts and maker education, school–community partnerships, youth empowerment, and young people's engagement with digital media. She is co-instructor (with Edward P. Clapp) of the online course Thinking and Learning in the Maker-Centered Classroom. She has presented her research in numerous presentations and publications. Jennifer is a former education chair and commissioner for the Maine Arts Commission and has assumed advisory and board roles for other nonprofit institutions. She has a background in education, art history, museum education and, prior to joining Project Zero, held educational leadership positions in arts organizations.

Shari Tishman, Ed.D.

Shari Tishman is a lecturer at Harvard Graduate School of Education and a senior research associate at Harvard Project Zero, where she recently served as director. Her research focuses on the development of thinking and understanding, the role of close observation in learning, and learning in and through the arts. She currently codirects Agency *by* Design, and also Out of Eden Learn, an online learning community that is currently being used in over 1200 classrooms worldwide and is linked to *National Geographic* journalist Paul Salopek's seven-year walk around the world. Past notable projects include Visible Thinking, a dispositional approach to teaching thinking that foregrounds the use of thinking routines and the documentation of student thinking, and Artful Thinking, a related approach that emphasizes the development of thinking dispositions through looking at art. The author of numerous articles and books, her forthcoming book, *The Power of Slow Looking*, will be published in 2017 by Routledge.

Thinking and Learning in the Maker-Centered Classroom

An online course exploring the potential of maker-centered learning from the perspective of the Agency *by* Design research initiative at Project Zero

Offered jointly by Project Zero and the Programs in Professional Education at the Harvard Graduate School of Education

Over the past decade, maker-centered classrooms and maker-centered learning have become increasingly popular. Young people (and teachers and parents alike) have greater opportunities than ever before to build, hack, redesign, and tinker with a variety of materials in school- or community-based spaces, design thinking and engineering programs, and at Maker Faires.

Maker-centered learning not only offers opportunities to learn about new tools and technologies, it requires certain thinking skills—such as navigating uncertainty, adaptability, collaborative thinking, risk-taking, and multiple-perspective taking—that are critical to engaging and thriving in a complex world.

Drawing on research from Project Zero's Agency *by* Design project, this online course offers classroom teachers, maker educators, administrators, and parents an opportunity to explore firsthand maker-centered learning practices and the opportunities they afford. Discover what kinds of tools might best support this kind of teaching and learning, and examine the benefits (to both young people and facilitators) of engaging in this work. Through hands-on, collaborative activities, consider how maker-centered learning experiences might fit into your home teaching and learning context.

To register and learn more, please visit: http://hvrd.me/9omT302fujU